Becoming a DIAMOND

OWN YOUR *brilliance* & REWRITE YOUR STORY

Becoming a DIAMOND

OWN YOUR *brilliance* & REWRITE YOUR STORY

NICOLE LINDHORST

Niche Press
Indianapolis, IN

DIAMOND JOURNAL

FOR DEEPER REFLECTION

On each Spark page in this book, I've given you space to reflect, journal, and take action. However, for even more reflection and transformation, I've also created **a free, downloadable journal with 118 prompts** to think about in addition to the questions in this book. If you'd like to dig deeper during your journey, scan this QR code to download your free copy.

NicoleLindhorst.com/Toolkit

*This book is dedicated to any woman who has ever felt like
she was not enough or who has always felt like she must validate
herself. My prayer for you is that you can move past the victim
mindset or simply recognize that it's ok to change the trajectory of
your story. You can break the cycle. Also know that God made you
for greater things and that you are always enough in His eyes.
And to the little girl who I was, who just wanted to be seen and
appreciated — and who grew up into a woman who made it possible.
And to my daughter, Emma, the inspiration for this book.
You are the light of my life. You make me see myself differently
and encourage me to be better. You are an amazing woman,
and I'm so proud of you!*

TABLE OF CONTENTS

A SIMPLE MENTAL SHIFT CAN CHANGE YOUR LIFE

It was May 2023, and our home was filled with excitement for my daughter Emma's graduation party. We had decorated, set up food, and prepared to celebrate her big day. I was just about to call down the stairs to check on her when she appeared.

She wore a simple white dress, a sash that read, *"I Graduated,"* and a diamond tiara, which perched proudly on her head. Her smile stretched from ear to ear as she twirled for me. Through teary eyes, I captured the moment on video, though it would be etched in my heart forever.

All day, people asked if she was excited about her next adventure, moving to Omaha for school. She hugged them, laughing, her eyes glowing with eagerness. But then, she wrapped me in a side hug and whispered, "Are you ready too, Mom?"

I nearly lost it. The question hit me in so many ways at once. And each of them held a different side of the truth.

No. I wasn't ready.

I couldn't tell her that, though — or even show it. Inside, I was fighting the tears. I didn't want to look weak. I didn't want anyone to question me or, worse, make me feel like I should not feel this way. My husband always says it's great to raise your kids and see them graduate, go to college, or know what they will do for a career. The goal is to get them out of your basement! And while I agree with that, as a mom, that didn't make this any easier, especially because the moment had truly snuck up on me.

Emma wasn't just my daughter. She was my friend too, someone who I know inside and out, and who also "got me." We could talk about things and know it was safe with each other. And if I'm honest, someone I may have confided in too much at times because she was honest and could tell me if I was overreacting. Right or wrong, my mom and I had the same kind of relationship before I got married. We shared a lot with each other too. So, I loved it when I was the one Emma often asked for advice late at night with her friends gathered around. She was woven into my daily purpose.

And soon, she would be gone. I was so damn proud of her, and I didn't want to create any doubt in her mind. I didn't want her to see me upset or feel like she needed to comfort me because I was "losing it." (And I type that with a smile on my face because it sounds so dramatic, but if you've been there, you know exactly what it feels like. Everything is fine, but we are just "slightly" overreacting in the moment.)

Motherhood hadn't just been something I did. It had been a place where I felt purposeful, anchored, essential. And when that role shifted, it exposed something I hadn't realized was there — a thin layer of fear. Maybe I had poured so much of myself into everyone else that I hadn't fully tended to who I was becoming aside from them. Can you relate?

I didn't allow myself to fully connect with that fear until a few months later, after we moved her into her new place. For the first time in 18 years, she wasn't under my roof. No goodnight kiss. No "Mom, come downstairs." Just... silence.

I crawled into bed and let the tears come, reminding myself that raising children to spread their wings was the goal. The knowledge didn't make that moment easier.

A PAINFUL QUESTION

That night, after I'd calmed down a little and my mind was spinning through the usual checklist (Did I lock the door? Did I turn off the stove? Did I feed the dog?), a deeper question sank in. If Emma doesn't need me the same way anymore, who am I?

Would she still call me when she was sad, or would she hide it and struggle alone? Was I worrying too much? (I have to admit, I loved the text I got shortly after she moved into her new place, with a photo of the new wooden block sign displayed on her shelf in the main room that said, "Call your MOM." That was, literally, a good sign.)

Still, the worries about Emma seemed to create a deeper question, one that went beyond just being a mom. Not just missing Emma. But confronting the space where I hadn't been asking the big question.

What's my purpose now?

That question didn't seem to have a ready answer. And even its presence hurt. The fear of irrelevance and loss of daily significance made me confront parts of myself that motherhood had caused me to postpone examining. For a moment, I wondered if my best work had already happened.

With these thoughts weighing on me, I did what I always did when faced with pain — I got busy. That was no problem. Since age 13, I'd carried multiple jobs, and by this time, I was running four businesses. If I wasn't working, I was volunteering or spending time helping others. I had always been the friend people came to for encouragement; the one others could confide in. I thought a full calendar meant a full life.

But deep down, I knew something felt off. Maybe the fear that came from missing Emma was trying to give me permission to think about myself again. I was in some kind of identity crisis, but it didn't make sense.

What am I missing?

I kept asking myself. On the surface, everything seemed good. I loved my businesses. I had a beautiful family and good friends, whom I also loved. And yet, I had an ache I couldn't ignore, a feeling underneath everything. More reflection brought a quiet message.

You were made for more.

I strongly believed this was true, but I had never given myself permission to really consider it. As a result, I had never had the space to honor the feeling and act on it. And even now, when I did, it remained a puzzle.

What? What is the "more"?

I didn't yet know how to find out — but I would.

A GIFT OF CHANGE

One day, around five months after Emma's move, I received a gift that would change everything: tuition from a Nebraska organization to spend on my personal growth. I chose a retreat at Sedona Mago.

For four days, I peeled back layers I had carried for decades. I examined my childhood roles of fixer, peacekeeper, and seeker of validation. I faced the patterns I'd absorbed from my parents' divorce and from growing up too fast. The self-work at the retreat made me realize something important — my natural skills of empathy and discernment could be both a blessing and a curse. Though they helped me understand and help others, they had also led me to carry others' pain as my own, at my own expense.

I realized that because of the roles I automatically took, I had become caught in a cycle. I had been trying so hard for years to avoid conflict, not wanting to make people feel hurt emotionally, that I had not considered my own feelings as equally important. And I realized others may not have even realized that their words were hurtful to me... because I had never told them.

I finally understood: *Hurt people hurt people.*

To break the cycle of being hurt and not moving forward, I pushed myself to have some hard conversations, ones I had avoided for years. I finally began asking questions to understand how my childhood relationships affected who I am today, how I react to change, and how I show up for myself. I was ready to break out of my negative patterns — for myself, for my family, and for the women I would one day serve.

I didn't know it until then that the brokenness I felt was not my own, but an emotion that had been projected onto me by others in their own emotional distress, and which I had accepted without realizing it wasn't mine. That realization has helped me to prepare for the coaching I would one day do.

And in that moment, I realized that coaching was what I wanted to do — the "more" I had been missing. It was my purpose in this next phase of my life. And I realized it wasn't so much about what I would be doing, but who I was becoming. I was stepping into a different sense of myself — one I didn't quite know yet but was curious to explore.

BREAKING FREE OF THE OLD ME

After that retreat, I knew I couldn't go back to "busy" as usual. I now felt like I had alternatives to some of my patterns, and I knew I wanted to go into coaching, but I honestly didn't know what to do next.

And the previous "me" questioned the change. What if I made a mistake? What if it didn't work? What was the "right" next step? What if people judged me for wanting too much? After all, I already had so many blessings. Was I ungrateful?

As I worked through these fears, my business coach asked me some hard questions. One of them was: "What is getting in the way of making the choice to become the version of you that God put you here to be?" As we talked through those answers, I realized the truth: The only thing standing in my way was me. My fear had me paralyzed. Yet any step toward my goal was right. All I needed to do was allow myself to get out of the cycle of fear I'd been caught in.

I thought hard about my four businesses: My rhinestone business felt sacred because it was my brand, but I wasn't "working" it anymore, so it was just another thing to do. The sign business was something I did to be creative and bring joy to others, but it too, was just another thing to do.

And then there was my clothing boutique. For seven years, it had been more than a store. It was where women came to find clothes, yes, but also to find friendship, laughter, and someone who would listen.

And my wellness studio, where I worked with women in so many different ways, helping them build their confidence and personal brand through color and style choices. I loved every minute there, too.

Yet God was calling me to do something different. And I was listening.

Did these businesses have a part in who I was becoming?

I decided to sell the sign and rhinestone businesses. That felt great. By releasing them to two wonderful women who said YES and would bring life back to the purpose and joy those businesses offered, I could give a gift to all of us and create the space to honor the deeper purpose stirring in me.

Then, I made one of the hardest choices: I closed my clothing boutique.

It felt like I was closing a chapter of myself. However, I knew that while the boutique brought value to others, it was no longer bringing *me* value. God was calling me into something bigger, and I was anxious to learn what it was. I wanted to be open to listening and strong enough to move forward with what I heard God calling me to do next.

I did decide to keep my BeYOUtiful brand. Instead of my boutique, I have now started BeYOUtiful Wellness Studio, combining it within the same place where I did my color and stylist work. Now, I was honoring what I had always been doing: helping people look and feel good from the outside in *and* the inside out. I wanted to officially expand those services even more to include the coaching I had been unofficially doing for years.

The transition wasn't easy. My old patterns — the need for being busy, the fear of being judged for trying to be "too much," the feeling that I had to justify my worth — followed me into this new chapter.

I had lived for years believing my ideas were silly or excessive, that my dreams were too big. The undermining inner voice haunted me. Why couldn't I just be content with these things now being gone? Why am I looking at doing something new?

And when I succeeded, I sometimes felt celebrated but not fully supported. Have you ever felt that way? Even in marriage, though my husband loved me, emotional support wasn't his strength. I often felt like I was dreaming alone.

Anchoring our identities in the titles we carry can make us feel stuck in this or that role or unsure what to do when the titles change. It can be difficult to move on.

However, with coaching and prayer, I began to rewrite the story. I was not *just* a boutique owner. I was not *just* a mom. While those titles were very important, I was not defined specifically by them. When they shifted, so could I. I would not break. I could look ahead and have big dreams and aspirations to be more and do more, and I didn't have to apologize or be afraid of being too much or desiring too much. I was exactly enough. God had called me to a greater purpose, and I was open to what HE had been shaping me for — and that openness would help me help other women see the greatness in themselves too.

BECOMING, NEVER BROKEN

On my phone, I created an album called "I Am Enough." It's filled with screenshots of encouraging messages from friends, clients, strangers, and most importantly, my family. Notes that say, "I see you. I'm proud of you. You've changed my life."

Every time I read them, I'm reminded: I was never broken. I was only becoming. And I am right where I need to be.

And nothing compares to the fire I feel when I'm speaking—whether on a stage or in a small group. The butterflies in my stomach, the Holy Spirit's whispers of what people need to hear, the joy of watching someone light up with clarity and hope.

This is my purpose — not just what I'm doing but *who I am becoming*. I am a speaker, a teacher, and a guide. I help women rediscover their brilliance and know their worth. I was already doing this in so many ways, even as I ran all my businesses. I already *was* this. I just needed to recognize the truth underneath all my daily activity.

WHAT'S MISSING FOR *YOU?*

If you're holding this book, you're probably not a beginner in life, either. You've lived. You've built a life. You've carried others. You've checked every box you were told would make you fulfilled.

And yet... something feels missing. Not broken — *missing*. A piece of you. A spark. A certainty. A voice you used to know. A dream that keeps resurfacing.

You might be in a season where you've outgrown the life you worked so hard to build. You feel scattered with ideas but tired of always being the strong one. You're proud of who you've been... yet you're craving more. You've hit a transition — empty nest, career shift, identity shift, or just that quiet inner voice, asking, "Is this all there is?" You're doing everything right, but it no longer feels aligned. You've lost yourself a little in the roles you've mastered.

And somewhere deep inside, you know:

There is more for you. Not just in what you are doing, but in who you are. Right now. Even if you don't see it yet.

That is why this book found you.

The fact is, no one taught you how to reinvent yourself in the middle of your life. No one prepared you for the moment when your identity, your purpose, your energy, your confidence, and your relationships would all shift at once. And yet, you have everything you need. You ARE everything you need.

THIS BOOK IS DESIGNED FOR YOU

This book isn't here to fix you — it's here to **reintroduce you to yourself.**

It will help you to name the quiet things you've been carrying. Untangle the thoughts that have kept you stuck. Rebuild your clarity and confidence. This book is meant to help you hear God's whisper beneath the noise, become the woman you've always felt you were meant to be, and step into a life that finally feels like yours again.

Your transformation happens through **7 Facets** — the very same ones I had to walk through myself. These are created in a framework of layers, as I've noted below.

Part 1: The **core/inner knowing** that makes up who you are (how God created you)

1. **Identity:** *How can I understand who I am now?*
2. **Purpose:** *How can I understand why I am here?*

Part 2: The way you **accept and express** yourself

3. **Self-Worth:** *How can I tell if I'm good enough?*
4. **Authenticity:** *How can I feel comfortable with who I am?*

Part 3: How you choose the **external actions, priorities, and connections/people** that can help you fulfill your purpose:

5. **Decisiveness:** *How can I learn to trust myself?*
6. **Focus:** *How can I stop feeling so scattered?*
7. **Relationship:** *How can I feel more supported?*

Part 4: The culmination of your **overall mastery of all of the layers,** the whole greater than the sum of its parts:

8. **Brilliance:** *How can I feel comfortable owning and sharing my gifts with others to help them shine too?*

THE STRUCTURE IS INTENTIONAL

Each Facet contains an introduction to help you understand what it represents, as well as a scripture to remind you that you are never alone. God is with you always, and He wants you to lean on Him. And when you do, you'll feel that transformation more clearly too.

For each Facet, you'll find eight Sparks of Wisdom — real, relatable moments from life — as well as a prompt to **Reflect** (to unlock clarity) and an action to help you **Polish** this Facet. You'll find a "sticky note" space to journal at the end of each **Spark**. (I always feel rude writing directly in a book, preferring to use sticky notes instead so I don't ruin the pages. If you're like me, you'll find space for your own sticky notes, so you feel you have permission to make the notes you need.)

We all love a great self-help book, but how many do you have that don't encourage action? My goal at the end of the Sparks is to offer you a guide to reflect and ACT! And as you continue through the whole book, you can see how you're becoming a diamond.

READ IN THE ORDER THAT FEELS RIGHT FOR YOU

Everything about this book is created specifically to help you achieve real change. With that in mind, I first want to free you to read it *in the way you need to.*

Trust what pulls at your heart. Feel free to start at whatever Facet (or Spark!) you like, even if they're not in order. Transformation doesn't happen in a rigid, one-size-fits-all sequence. Pick up where it feels the most needed.

SAVOR EACH FACET AND SPARK ONE BY ONE

This book isn't meant to be rushed — it's meant to be *felt*. You don't need to read it in an afternoon. Instead, open to the story or lesson that resonates with where you are today, and give yourself the gift of slowing down long enough to reflect, journal, and take the action step.

Focus on each Facet or Spark of Wisdom on its own, in the moment you need it most. Just as with a butterfly in its cocoon, you can't speed up the process by cutting open the cocoon for the butterfly to emerge. If you do, the butterfly won't survive. It needs to go through the process as God intended, and so do you.

COMMIT TO TAKING ACTION

More than simple inspiration, the material in this book is a self-guided process, layered with coaching, reflection, and spiritual grounding. It's not just another self-help read that doesn't ask you to take any action.

However, I also don't want you to feel overwhelmed. With that in mind, I've included actions that are simple yet impactful. Most people assume that worthwhile changes have to be huge, but that's just not true. Little steps can make a big impact — what matters is that *you take action.*

My hope is that if you follow these guidelines, by the end, you won't just understand the framework... You'll feel the shift. You'll see yourself differently, move differently, and choose differently as understanding sets in.

You were never lost or broken. You were becoming.

And this book — *Becoming a Diamond* — is the gift I get to share with you. It is your reminder that diamonds aren't destroyed by pressure — they're created by it.

And so are you.

DOWNLOAD YOUR *DIAMOND JOURNAL* FOR DEEPER REFLECTION

On each Spark page in this book, I've given you space to reflect, journal, and take action. However, for even more reflection and transformation, I've also created **a free, downloadable journal with 118 prompts** to think about in addition to the questions in this book. If you'd like to dig deeper during your journey, scan this QR code to download your free copy.

NicoleLindhorst.com/Toolkit

IT'S HARD TO BELIEVE SOMETHING SO BEAUTIFUL STARTS OUT AS A LUMP OF DARK, UNREMARKABLE-SEEMING MATERIAL BURIED DEEP UNDER THE EARTH.

PART 1

Inner Knowing

Did you know that diamonds form from coal? It's hard to believe something so beautiful starts out as a lump of dark, unremarkable-seeming material buried deep under the earth.

This first set of Facets is like that coal. It's the raw, pressurized beginning in which the truths that are already there are waiting to shine. Here, you will slow down and return there, exploring *who you are* at your core, the truth beneath the roles, responsibilities, and expectations you've carried, beneath ideas of who you were ten years ago or who others needed you to be. You will begin rediscovering your gifts and values and reconnect with *why you are here and what it means now,* in this season of your life.

This is the work of remembering. You'll learn to ground, or re-ground, your identity internally instead of borrowing it from titles or approval. As you move through this section, expect reflection, clarity, and a few realizations that, though uncomfortable at first, will ultimately steady you. Before a diamond can shine outwardly, it must first be known to itself, to its own inner light, even when it is in the dark.

IDENTITY

You are fearfully and wonderfully made. — Psalm 139:14

"Who am I outside all the roles I play?"

Identity confusion happens quietly.

One day, you're living the life you built, managing schedules, taking care of others, showing up, achieving, and serving. Then a moment arrives that makes you pause. It might be someone's graduation. A career shift. A child growing up. Or even just a changing season.

Whatever the trigger, suddenly, you feel something you can't quite name.

That's what happened to me.

As I mentioned in my story about why I wrote this book, before my trigger moment, I thought I knew who I was — a wife, a mom, a business owner. But when my daughter walked across that graduation stage, something inside me whispered, *"There's a part of you you've been ignoring."*

That part wanted space and recognition. And I suddenly realized I hadn't checked in with it for years.

The same thing happened when I closed my boutique and sold my rhinestone and sign businesses. I didn't just lose responsibilities — I lost pieces of the identity I had built my entire adult life around.

For years, I believed that what I did was who I was. And when what I did changed, I wasn't sure who I was anymore.

RESOLVING IDENTITY CONFUSION

Since you're reading this, it's probably safe to assume that you might have some of these struggles, too. You've been moving through your life when suddenly, something changes. It could be a drastic shift or a subtle, internal one. Whether it's prompted by external or internal forces, the view of yourself that you've had for years seems threatened or inadequate, and you're not sure what to do now.

What Identity Issues Feel Like

If you're struggling with issues related to your identity, you may feel:

- Uncertain how to define who you are beyond your roles.
- A little empty, even if life looks full.
- Restless, disconnected, or "off."
- Like you've focused so hard on knowing everyone else, you've forgotten yourself.
- Tired of shaping yourself by necessity instead of your real desires.

And you might find yourself asking, "Who am I when the titles fade?" "What do *I* want?" or "What part of me have I forgotten?"

What Polishing this Facet Helps Bring

Working on this Facet will help you:

- Feel grounded and secure in who you are.
- Reconnect with your desires, values, and voice.
- Discover the woman behind the roles.
- Feel whole, not scattered.
- Show up with confidence that comes from self-trust.
- Know your identity is *rooted*, not borrowed.
- Have confidence without needing a title to justify it.

Over time, you will understand who you are and what gifts and talents God has placed in you to share with others, helping you to really understand who you are now. You will gain a new mindset, shifting your identity from what others expect of you to what you want, with or without the roles or titles you hold.

How We'll Get There

The eight Sparks of Wisdom in this Facet will guide you through the quiet rediscovery of who you really are. They'll help you:

- Remember the parts of you that you've forgotten.
- Recognize the woman God created beneath the roles.
- Understand the shifts happening inside you.
- Rebuild a sense of self that feels authentic, grounded, and whole.

This is the beginning of coming home to yourself.
Let's begin.

A rough, uncut diamond looks like an ordinary stone — no sparkle, no dazzling shine. Only when unearthed, cut, and polished do its facets reveal the brilliance inside. And you are no different. While life's layers, such as roles, responsibilities, and expectations, may have hidden your sparkle, you are valuable. Your brilliance is waiting to be unearthed, shaped, polished. You don't need to become someone new. You just need to rediscover the woman who has always been inside you.

RECOGNIZE WHEN "BROKEN IN" HAS BECOME "WORN OUT"

Like your favorite pair of jeans — the ones you've worn so many times they've molded to you — your daily routines and the roles you play can feel the same. Broken in. Comfortable. Familiar.

And when you're used to wearing a certain pair of jeans, you feel a little less put together when they're in the laundry, and you're forced to reach for a different pair. It throws you off, and your confidence isn't as strong. The alternate pair might not fit quite right, and you make excuses for why you don't look put together.

Then there are the seasons when even your favorite jeans stop fitting the way they used to — thanks to that inevitable 5 or 10-pound roller coaster we all ride. Suddenly, they're tight in places they never were before. They rub. They pinch. The growth creates friction. And again... you feel off balance, unsure.

Life works the exact same way.

Just like with those jeans, you feel a little less put together or somewhat thrown off when a role no longer seems to fit quite the same. It's become worn out, or you've changed a little. You're forced to reach for a different one that's not broken in as well, not as comfortable. It doesn't feel quite right, either.

Yes — we can outgrow our roles. Our identities shift. Titles we've worn with pride — wife, mom, business owner, leader, fixer, the dependable one — begin to feel just a little too snug.

This shift can feel confusing. Nothing is wrong, but something isn't right. Your responsibilities are the same. Your routines are the same. From the outside, life might look identical. Yet inside, something is stretching. Expanding. Making room.

If this is happening to you, for the first time, you may sense a new realization rising:

**These roles aren't broken...
but they're not all of me anymore.**

It's the quiet signal that God is growing you into the woman you're becoming, and the old roles simply can't hold her anymore.

Fearing this signal means failure, you may want to fight it. However, there's another option: You can replace fear with curiosity and choose to listen. Understand that it's actually a sign of potential transformation, a holy invitation into what's coming next. Are you feeling it? Are you ready to accept the invitation and see where it leads?

When the roles you've worn with pride start to feel tight, it's not failure — it's growth. God is expanding you beyond what once fit, inviting you into the next version of who you're meant to be.

 **Reflect:** What shift in your identity has left you uneasy lately? Could it be that this change is not an ending, but the polishing of a new facet of your own brilliance? If you could remove all expectations, what version of yourself have you quietly longed to step into?

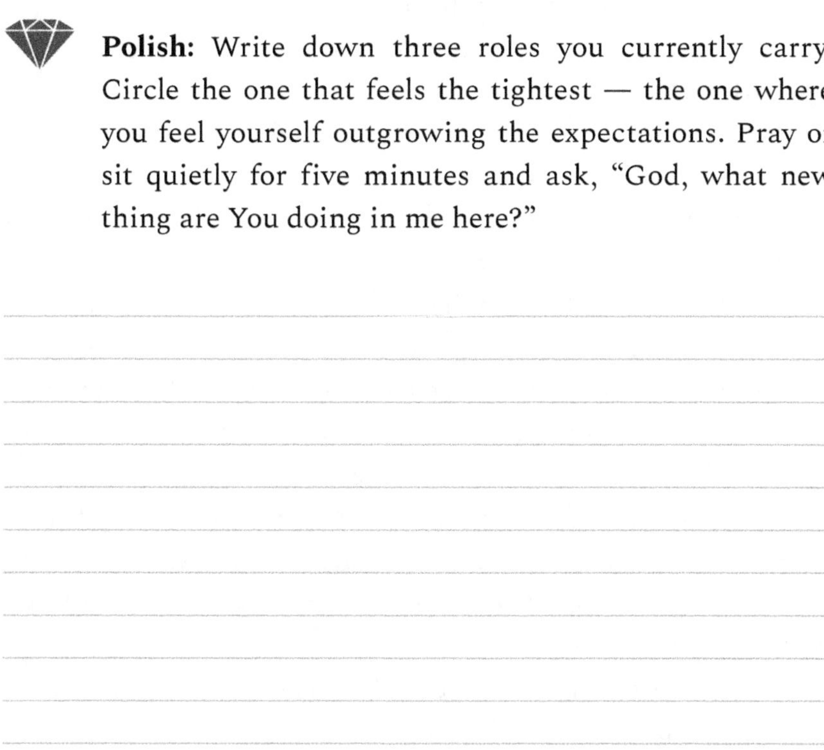 **Polish:** Write down three roles you currently carry. Circle the one that feels the tightest — the one where you feel yourself outgrowing the expectations. Pray or sit quietly for five minutes and ask, "God, what new thing are You doing in me here?"

SEE TITLES AS SEASONS

What do you do when a job, business, or title you've carried for years suddenly isn't yours anymore, and you wonder who you are without it?

When you've poured your heart into something for so long that it is woven into the way you introduce yourself, the way you fill your days, and the way you see your worth, its ending feels like the loss of a part of yourself — even when you were the one who decided to end it. No matter how much the mind says, "This is right. This is good," the heart quietly grieves the loss of what the title once meant.

In that mindset, you've been looking at the title as an identity. Instead, what if you think of it more as a season?

That perspective feels different somehow.

Seasons naturally flow into each other. Every *ending* brings something *new*. In our lives, **the endings of different titles or roles bring new clarity you can't embrace while still holding on to the past.**

When every shift makes room for the woman you're becoming, why wouldn't you welcome those changes?

You are not defined only by the work you've done. You are also shaped by the courage it took to grow through it. That courage hasn't left simply because the work is changing.

Even when change is our choice, it can feel like failure.
Yet titles don't define us; what we do with our gifts and
passions in this moment does.

Reflect: What title are you holding onto so tightly that it's keeping you from stepping into your next chapter of happiness? Could letting go be making a cut in your Diamond that allows your light to shine through it more brightly?

Polish: Take one action today to explore or try on a new version of yourself, outside of that old title.

CLEAR OUT YOUR "ROLE CLOSET"

"I have NOTHING to wear."

Most women have said this while standing in a closet that's full of clothes from past seasons, past roles, and past versions of themselves. And it makes perfect sense because we know the frustration isn't really about clothes. It's about *identity.*

Identity works the same as your frustrating closet. You can have a life overflowing with roles — mom, wife, leader, helper, achiever — and still feel like nothing fits anymore because you've outgrown how you've been showing up.

At some point, many women stop choosing from within themselves and start choosing from the expectations of others (whether real or imagined). What's practical? What won't draw attention? What keeps the peace?

And over time, those externally-based choices create quiet disconnection.

The breakthrough doesn't come from finding the "right outfit." It comes from asking a deeper question: **What am I choosing from — my true self or the roles I learned to survive in?**

When I invested in defining my own style and color, the new clothes didn't give me identity — they reflected what was already there. My choices, free to come from within me, were very different than what I had been wearing. The difference revealed how often I had been living from who I thought I *should* be, not who I actually was.

This Spark is about something similar — your "identity wardrobe." It's about reclaiming your authority to choose your roles and activities from *within yourself* again.

Identity isn't about roles — it's the source of your choices. When you keep doing the same things without checking whether they reflect your true self, life can feel like a full closet with nothing that fits. Somewhere along the way, you may have stopped choosing from who you really are.

Reflect: What makes you feel complete? Where have you stopped expressing your authentic self? What little sparkle could you add to your day to honor who you truly are?

Polish: Pick one small way today to express yourself — through clothing, a hobby or activity, or even a mindset shift.

AWAKEN TO WHO YOU'RE BECOMING

Close your eyes for a moment and imagine yourself on a dream vacation — or even just a quiet weekend away. No schedules. No carpools. No laundry piles, work demands, or family obligations tugging at your sleeve.

Just you.

Now picture the woman you become in that space.

Does she hang her clothes neatly with care or let them drape freely across the chair because she's finally relaxed enough not to care?

Does she wander to breakfast in her favorite cozy sweater, order room service, or slip into a quiet corner of a café with a glass of wine, savoring every moment without feeling rushed?

Does she rise early to greet the sunrise... or stay up late, letting the stillness of the night wrap around her like a gentle blanket?

Does she flip on the TV for background comfort... or leave the silence untouched, finally able to hear her own thoughts again?

This woman — the one who emerges when life loosens its grip — is not a stranger. She is you, beneath the roles, routines, and responsibilities.

And you don't have to wait for a vacation to meet her again.

She's already within you, ready to reconnect with the rest of yourself that's been buried under busyness.

When you imagine life without the pull of responsibility, you catch a glimpse of who you are underneath it all. Freedom has a way of revealing the parts of your identity you've set aside.

Reflect: What does freedom feel like to you? What brings you joy? Where has that version of yourself been hiding, and how can you allow her light to shine again, polished and brilliant like a diamond waiting to reflect its full radiance? Who are you when no one else is relying on you?

Polish: Today, take one action that honors that *true self,* even in a small way.

RECLAIM WHAT SPARKS JOY

Somewhere between the carpool lines, calendars, careers, and caring for everyone else, we forget the things that once made us feel alive. We never stop wanting them, but life got busy.

In my teens, I spent summer after summer detasseling and rouging just to buy a guitar. I remember the thrill of finally holding it in my hands. Lessons weren't affordable, and though a few of my mom's friends showed me some chords, I never really learned to play.

Decades later, I still own that guitar. And every time I'm at a live concert, watching musicians lose themselves in the music, something inside me stirs. My heart whispers, "I wish I could do that."

People say, "Just learn! You have YouTube. You have access. You can afford it now." And they're right. There's nothing stopping me — except that the spark to start hasn't fully returned.

But the desire? It's still alive. Quiet, steady, persistent. Waiting for the right time.

Do you have something like that guitar?

It could be a dream you once held. A hobby you loved. A talent you pressed pause on because life demanded other things.

Identity confusion often starts right here — when the things that light us up get buried under the things that keep us busy. But desire is never accidental. It's a breadcrumb trail back to who you are.

Every year, I place that guitar on my dream board — a reminder that some dreams aren't gone... they're just waiting for us to turn toward them again.

Maybe this year is your year too.

Your "guitar" sits untouched — a quiet symbol of forgotten dreams. You begin to realize your identity isn't found only in your responsibilities, but also in the things that make you feel alive.

Reflect: What hobby or passion is still calling to you, waiting for your courage to pick it back up? Could revisiting it be a path to revealing more of your hidden brilliance?

Polish: Take one step today to reconnect with that hobby, passion, or interest.

REFLECT ON WHAT MATTERS MOST

There's something about reaching an age milestone — 30, 40, 45, 50 — that quietly changes the questions we ask ourselves. Maybe you used to look forward to them, wondering, "What's next?" Yet now, you catch yourself staring at the candles, wondering if your best days are behind you.

Maybe it's time for a different, more transformative question: "What matters now?"

Turning 40 made me ask that question. I realized I needed to reconnect with my core values. They hadn't changed, but the way I needed to live them had.

Core values don't disappear over time; however, they do get crowded out. Care, freedom, faith, creativity, connection, peace, purpose — they can all be quietly deprioritized while you're doing what needs to be done.

A milestone simply creates space to notice which values are asking to be re-expressed now. Reflecting on these questions doesn't mean you're ungrateful or dissatisfied. You're merely acknowledging that you've been living — serving, building, carrying responsibility — and somewhere along the way, your attention shifted to what was required instead of what was rooted in your values.

Milestones have a way of holding up a mirror.

They ask:

- What do I value most in this season?
- What am I giving my time and energy to?
- Does my life still reflect what matters to me — or is it mostly focused on what matters to others?

The answers bring clarity. Could it be that God is calling you to a new season of your life, with a new part of your identity waiting to be polished and revealed like a diamond just beginning to shine?

Remember: Identity isn't static. It evolves as your values move from survival to deeper intention. How has your identity evolved with age, experience, or major life events? As you cross the finish line of a milestone, what have you learned? How can you use it to express and reconnect with your values in a new way?

Thinking about those things can be much more exciting than looking back in regret, or simply asking, "What's next?" When you work from intention, what's next becomes what you choose, not just what happens to you.

Milestones don't change who you are — they clarify how you're meant to live now. Your values remain, but their expression evolves as you move from survival to intention.

Reflect: Which values feel most important to you in this season of life — and where have they been honored or overlooked? If your calendar reflected your values perfectly, what would look different?

Polish: Write down one deeply important thing to you that needs attention during this next season of your life. Now choose one specific activity you can do this week to embrace it.

RECALL THE CLUES OF WHO YOU'VE ALWAYS BEEN

Have you experienced this moment? You're flipping through an old photo album or scrolling past childhood pictures, and you suddenly come face to face with a little girl you barely recognize. A girl who lived without worry or fear of judgment.

You can almost see her again.

She's the one who lined up her dolls like an audience and put on concerts in the living room. Who decorated her room in whatever colors made her smile. Who mixed "lemonade" out of whatever she could find just so she could sell it on the driveway. Who invented games in the backyard, climbed where she shouldn't, chased lightning bugs, danced without rhythm, and didn't care one bit who was watching.

She was fearless. Creative. Unfiltered. Full of wonder. Wildly herself.

And then... somewhere along the way, life got louder. Experiences shaped her. People's opinions mattered more. Validation quietly replaced pure joy. Proving herself started to feel necessary. And that free little girl slowly learned to shrink.

You look at her in those old photos — the spark in her eyes, the unapologetic confidence — and you wonder: *Where did she go? And when did I stop being her?*

But... she didn't disappear. She's still in you. She's just layered under years of roles, expectations, responsibility, and the belief that who you are needs to be earned.

Your most authentic self isn't lost. She's waiting to be remembered.

*When you look back at your younger, fearless self,
you see how confidence slowly gave way to a desire for approval.
Somewhere along the way, your identity was shaped
more by expectations than by who you truly were.*

Reflect: Where did that fearless girl go? Which parts of your bold, authentic self have been lost along the way? How could reconnecting with her spirit and courage help you as you polish your Identity Facet?

Polish: Do one small thing today that reconnects you with that confident, authentic self.

RELEASE YOUR SURVIVAL SELVES

There are versions of us that we didn't choose from desire, but from necessity.

One version learned to be agreeable to keep the peace. Another became capable because no one else was. And then there's the one who stayed quiet because being "too much" felt risky.

These versions aren't wrong. The part of yourself that built them was wise. She was resourceful. She protected you. She helped you survive.

For me, these "survival versions" were shaped early. My parents' divorce, their own past experiences, and the circumstances around me required me to grow up faster. I became the dependable one. The strong one. The one people could count on.

And while becoming those things didn't define me, it absolutely shaped me.

That evolution taught me resilience, responsibility, empathy, and leadership. It formed values I still carry with gratitude today. Instead of feeling I was a victim of my upbringing, I saw it as a gift, one that helped shape the woman I am now.

However, survival is not the same as identity.

There comes a moment when what once kept you safe begins to feel heavy. Exhausting. Limiting. Meant for a season you no longer live in, it now no longer fits.

If you feel this way, it means you're outgrowing the version of you that was built to hold everything together.

So, what happens next? You don't have to reject who you were. Instead, why not thank her and choose how to use her strength with intention instead of habit?

You'll know when it's time to release the version of yourself that was built to survive. You can recognize that while she protected you, she is not who you are meant to remain. Identity clarity comes when you honor who you had to be, without letting her define who you choose to become.

Reflect: Which versions of you were built to survive — and how might God be inviting you to use their strength without carrying their weight anymore?

Polish: Write down one trait you're known for that sometimes feels exhausting. Ask yourself: *How can this gift serve others without costing me myself?*

PURPOSE

"For I know the plans I have for you... plans to prosper you and not to harm you, plans to give you a hope and a future." — Jeremiah 29:11

"I know I'm meant for more, but what is it?"

Purpose uncertainty doesn't always show up as a crisis — often, it comes as a whisper. A quiet ache. A sense that the life you're living is good... but not quite aligned with the life you're called to live.

This sense often surfaces in the still moments — in the car alone, at night, during prayer, in the silence after a busy season. That lingering question reappears.

"Is this it?"

In Sally's case, the question nearly shattered her.

She had learned early how to survive. Growing up in a broken home and moving through the foster care system, she learned to adapt, stay alert, and take care of herself. Even as a little girl, she knew one thing with certainty: When she grew up, she would be a mom, and she would never leave her child behind. That dream carried her through the hard seasons.

But after Sally got married, she learned she couldn't have children. Suddenly, the purpose she had clung to, which had given meaning to her pain, was gone.

Overwhelmed with grief at this double loss of both children and life meaning, she did what many capable women do when they don't know where to put their pain — she stayed busy.

She said yes to everything. Community events. Extra clients. Volunteering. Family responsibilities. She packed her calendar, putting her energy into whatever she could, telling herself she thrived in chaos.

Her busy life looked like generosity, but inside, Sally was just trying to survive. She didn't want to admit that she was really just avoiding the quiet times, when she would have to face her grief and her unanswered questions.

Eventually, she realized God was nudging her toward counseling, compassion, and a deeper connection with Him — and possibly, renewed purpose.

However, the enemy quickly began to whisper too.

You'll spend your life fixing everyone else. You'll still be alone. No one showed up for you — why keep giving yourself away?

Listening to these messages, Sally stayed in her cycle of chaos. Her energy remained scattered, unfocused.

The turning point came in an unexpected place — an airport. While sharing her story with a stranger, Sally explained her love for children and related a little about her grief and her chaotic life. The woman listened quietly, then asked one simple question:

"Why didn't you foster?"

Stunned, Sally didn't know how to answer.

The question cut through years of mental noise. As she pondered it, Sally suddenly realized she hadn't lost her purpose — she had been running from it. She needed to reset her intention and commit to achieving what she meant to do, no matter what obstacles she faced or what her negative inner voice told her.

As Sally began grounding herself in prayer — not just asking for direction, but for protection from the negative thoughts — she learned to recognize which thoughts were from God and which were not. She stopped filling every gap with activity and started aligning her energy with what mattered most.

By reconnecting with her purpose, she redeemed her grief, transforming it. Today, she is licensed and awaiting a placement call and couldn't be happier.

REDISCOVERING PURPOSE

Most of us have wrestled with the question of purpose in some way.

I've built businesses, sold businesses, chased opportunities, and created a full, beautiful life. On the outside, it all looked complete. But lying awake, I remember wondering:

"Why doesn't this feel like enough?"

For me, that question became the seed of this entire Facet. I gradually came to understand that the underlying problem related back to my purpose.

Purpose is not found in the busyness, the titles, or the accomplishments. It rests in discovering who you are meant to serve and how God asks you to show up in the world. Even success can feel empty when it's measured by old definitions. In the midst of all your achievements, you still hear that whisper: **"You were made for more."**

If you're thinking about what that "more" might be for you, that's a sign you may need to work on the Purpose Facet. Let's look at some other signs too.

What Unclear Purpose Feels Like

If you feel any of the following, you may be struggling with purpose:

- Restless, even when things are going well.
- Like something is missing, but you can't name it.
- Unsure of your next step or direction.
- Unfulfilled by things that used to inspire you.
- Pulled toward something bigger but unclear what it is.
- A quiet tug toward change that you can't explain.

What Polishing this Facet Will Bring

When you work on this Facet, you will:

- Feel more aligned with and connected to your calling.
- Understand who you're meant to serve.
- Identify what your gifts are pointing you toward.
- Feel confident in your next step(s).
- Move toward a sense of fulfillment that feels grounded, peaceful, and true.
- Find meaning that isn't tied to general achievement, but rather, to impact.

In short, you'll feel peace instead of pressure, conviction instead of doubt. Instead of moving restlessly without direction, you'll start moving forward with momentum.

How We'll Get There

The next eight Sparks of Wisdom will guide you through the questions that reveal your purpose — gently, honestly, and spiritually. You will:

- Recognize the desires God placed in you.
- Understand why you feel the tug for *more*.

- Identify what that sense of *more* is for you — the work that brings you life, not burnout.
- Move from uncertainty to aligned direction.
- Begin seeing your purpose with fresh clarity.

This isn't about reinventing yourself. It's about uncovering the truth that's been inside you all along.

Deep beneath the surface, a diamond already contains its potential. The cut does not create brilliance. It unlocks what is already there.

Purpose is not something you manufacture. It is something you uncover and unlock. When you stop measuring your life by titles and start measuring it by calling, you begin to see that the "more" you're longing for isn't outside of you. It has been embedded in you all along.

Purpose is the design God set in you before anyone else named you.

BECOME HER BEFORE YOU BUILD HER

High-capacity women often fall into a subtle trap when we think about purpose. We ask things like:

"What should I do next?"

"What opportunity should I take?"

"What decision moves me forward?"

I've done this myself. During certain seasons of my life, I prayed for direction, asking God to show me the next move. I wanted clarity on the *what*. But what I really needed was refinement in the *who*.

The problem is that the "what should I do?" mindset treats purpose like a task list. Though we don't realize it, this perspective sets us back because purpose isn't first about *what we do*. It's about *who we are* — and that includes *who we're becoming*.

Think about it. When you chase the right opportunity but are working from the wrong identity — a past role-based idea of yourself or a negative inner voice — or when you step into a calling before you've grown into the woman who can carry it, even success feels heavy. You may be able to do all the "tasks," but they feel overwhelming. Clarity comes when you stop asking *what you should do* and start asking *who you should become*.

The fact is that you don't rise to the level of your opportunity. You rise to the level of your identity. Imagine a ceiling stopping your growth — that's what your identity can become if you let it. You need to raise your identity ceiling so your purpose can rise too.

Shifting the question from "What should I do?" to "Who do I need to become to steward what I'm asking for?" changes everything. Instead of chasing more visibility, you cultivate integrity. Instead of pursuing influence, you strengthen character. Instead of demanding clarity before you take the leap, you practice courage by leaping even when you can't see exactly where.

Collecting roles won't help you define your purpose. You clarify your purpose as you refine your character. You don't need a louder sign from God. You just need a deeper alignment within yourself.

Purpose becomes clearer when you focus less on what to do and more on who you are becoming. If you stop chasing the next opportunity and instead, start shaping the woman who can carry it, your "identity ceiling" rises, opening new opportunities for your purpose.

Reflect: Where in your life are you asking God for answers — are you striving for a new role, platform, result? Could the real invitation perhaps be a call to first grow in courage, integrity, or capacity?

Polish: Set aside five minutes today for silence. No phone, no drama, no multitasking. Simply sit and ask: **"God, what do You want me to notice today?"** Then write down whatever stirs in your spirit.

TUNING IN WORKS BETTER THAN CHASING

Maybe you've felt it — that restless ache that shows up even when life looks successful from the outside. The jobs, the titles, the businesses, the busy schedule... and yet something inside still feels unfinished.

I know that feeling well.

Since I was thirteen, I have worked nonstop — always adding a new job, a new project, a new business. I told myself it was ambition, but underneath, I was searching for something I could not name. When dissatisfaction crept in, I would simply move on to the next thing. It looked like drive, but it felt like emptiness.

It took years and some burnout to realize what was really happening: I wasn't chasing success. I was chasing purpose.

And no matter how high I climbed, it never felt like I had "made it."

What finally shifted everything was learning to slow down long enough to listen. Instead of focusing on building my résumé, I turned my attention toward noticing the types of work that actually brought deep contentment —moments when I felt useful, aligned, connected, and exactly who God created me to be.

That's when purpose started to come into focus. The purpose I was intended for had shaped everything about me, including what interests and satisfies me most. Tuning in to those things helped me more closely align with that deep inner core of purpose within me.

It's the same for you. Your restlessness is a sign that God is redirecting you toward the work that was always meant for you. When you stop chasing the next thing for your résumé and start tuning in to the next right thing for who you really are, purpose finally feels like peace.

Fulfillment isn't found in the next opportunity; it's discovered when we stop running long enough to listen. The pause you have been resisting might just be the doorway to your purpose.

Reflect: Where in your life are you chasing validation instead of true purpose? Where are you seeking fulfillment outside of what really matters to you?

Polish: List one thing today that would bring genuine joy or satisfaction, and commit to taking a first small step toward it this week.

CREATE SPACE TO RECONNECT WITH YOUR PURPOSE

Maybe you've had a season when your calendar was packed from edge to edge — kids' schedules, work demands, commitments, responsibilities. You ran, ran, ran and you kept telling yourself you thrive in the chaos, or that being busy means being valuable. In your eyes, movement means purpose.

Until one day... it doesn't.

I lived that too. For years, I filled every hour, convinced the pace proved something about who I was. And when I finally slowed down — closed businesses, cleared space in the calendar, signed off of the "Mom Taxi" and had all the kids driving — the silence felt terrifying. In it was the quiet inner accusation: **"You're not doing enough." "You're falling behind."** You may know that voice well. Most women do.

Yet in that uncomfortable pause when the noise stops, your true purpose finally has room to speak too. The world won't fall apart if you step back. Your worth won't evaporate if your schedule opens up. Your calling won't disappear if you stop running.

The empty pages in your life hold an invitation: a sacred opening for clarity, joy, and meaning to rise again.

And maybe that's exactly what your soul has been asking for. So, when you see a blank space in your calendar, instead of filling it up with another to-do item or volunteer shift, I would encourage you to take that gifted time to reflect. (And if you are looking for ways to do that, try some of the prompts in my free Diamond Journal. My gift to you! See the QR code in the back or front of the book if you haven't yet.)

An empty calendar isn't a failure; it's an invitation to rediscover what truly matters. Space allows purpose and joy to breathe.

Reflect: If your planner were empty, what new pages of purpose would you begin to write for yourself? What would your ideal day or week look like if you were living with purpose?

Polish: Pick one task, activity, or moment today that aligns with what truly matters to you and commit to doing it this week.

TAKE THE FIRST STEP AND THE REST WILL UNFOLD

Have you ever sat in church listening to the priest's homily and felt like it was directed right at you? It happens a lot to me. But one time was different — I had goosebumps on my arms, butterflies in my stomach, and tears filling my eyes. I knew this time, I needed to listen deeply.

I had been asking for answers, and I was open, really open, to hear what God wanted me to hear. And it was as clear as day.

The Holy Spirit filled my mind with the words, "I gave you many gifts and talents to share. Don't bury them because you are afraid. Afraid of the idea. Afraid of the opinions. Afraid of failure. I am with you always, and I will give you what you need."

The words pierced my heart. "You were made for great things. You can inspire so many people. You are kind, and you love others. You are empathetic and can listen to women who need you to hear them."

I felt it in my bones. But then came the harder part. What did that mean? What was I being called to do? Who was I being called to serve? And would anyone trust me enough to let me serve them?

Have you ever had a moment where you really felt God speaking to you but didn't know what it meant or how to move forward?

The call on our hearts is often an invitation to step out in faith before we see the full picture. Uncertainty doesn't mean you're not on the right path; it usually means God is guiding you one step at a time. You may not be able to see the next step, but it is there. If it's a vision or thought that you know didn't come from you, it's the Holy Spirit leading you. And if it keeps coming back, you know it's time to move!

God equips us for the calling before we fully see the path. Faith begins in the step, not in knowing it all before we start the journey.

Reflect: What gifts or callings have you been feeling on your heart, but have hesitated to act on out of fear? What gifts or talents has God given you that you might be holding back?

Polish: Choose one way today to use a gift you've been holding back. Even a small step counts.

YOUR GIFTS ARE CLUES TO YOUR CALLING

Think back to elementary school — before life got complicated, before responsibilities piled up, before you learned to
shrink or second-guess yourself. What did adults say about
you even then?

"She's a leader."

"She has a big voice."

"She always takes charge."

"She's so creative."

Those early observations weren't random; they were clues.

Sometimes, the things others notice don't feel like compliments or gifts. In second grade, my teacher told my mom
that students naturally followed my lead. At the time, the
statement felt awkward to me. I felt too old for my age, too
aware, too responsible. Life at home was shifting, and somewhere inside I believed leadership meant I had to carry the
weight. I didn't want that. What I didn't understand back
then (and what I want you to know now) is this: The traits you
carried as a child were not accidents — they were the earliest
signs of your purpose.

Remembering the stories, I realized they were all related
to skills I carried into adulthood. Being a leader as a child,
having empathy and speaking up for others, being the one to
take action when goals are set, and being able to take ideas
and make them tangible — those skills are still true about
me now.

I believe that if you really think back to these moments in
your own youth, they will show you the strengths you've had all

along: Leadership. Empathy. Curiosity. Creativity. Organization. Independence. Vision. These and/or whatever other gifts others may have noticed about you were woven into you long before life pulled you in a hundred directions.

Your childhood dreams weren't silly. Your hobbies weren't random. Your tendencies weren't flaws — they were seeds.

And if you look closely, you'll still see how those characteristics still show up today. They are the strengths you should lean on for your purpose.

Your calling is a gift that shows up early
and grows as you embrace your purpose.

Reflect: What did others notice about you as a child that you may have dismissed or seen as negative but could actually be pointing to your purpose today? What childhood dreams or passions hint at your true purpose?

Polish: Identify one way today to revisit or honor one of those early dreams.

SHIFT FROM *HOW* TO *WHO*

During a recent visit with my friend Jen, she shared that, like me, she has felt the desire for years now to help. To coach. To lead. She shared that she knows what she needs to do, but the question always comes back: *How?*

That question already feels overwhelming, and it doesn't help when, as a lot of us do, she finds herself scrolling through Facebook and Instagram, watching videos of all the women who seem to be doing exactly what she's dreamt of doing. So instead of being inspired, she feels small.

Jen started asking herself, "Why can't I do that? Why can't I figure this out? Why does it look so easy for them?"

Comparison doesn't just steal joy, it clouds purpose. The truth is, the more you scroll, the more you lose sight of your own unique gifts and voice. You're chasing others' paths instead of walking on your own.

God doesn't need you to be that other person who's doing what you want to do. He needs you to be you, doing your version of it in your way. **And the women you are meant to serve aren't looking for someone else's version of what they need; they're waiting for *the exact way that only you can show up.***

Sometimes, it takes exactly the right person at the right time to make a difference in someone's life. Right now, someone is praying for something they need, though they may not even know what it is. And you are the one who has exactly what they need. Not that other person who's doing what you want to do. You.

Why are you hesitating?

Comparing ourselves to others, it is easy to feel envy and self-doubt. They seem to have it all figured out. When we remember that God's plan is unique to each individual, we realize comparisons don't matter — what matters is that we offer the gifts we have, in our own special way.

Reflect: Are you scrolling and comparing, or are you creating and showing up in your own lane? Where are you comparing yourself and losing focus on your own purpose?

Polish: Today, write down one area where you can stop comparing and focus on your own path instead.

HONOR THE DEEP IMPACT IN SMALL MOMENTS

Some seasons of life are crazy — full schedules, busy homes, endless responsibilities. And then suddenly... things quiet down.

Maybe the kids are older. Maybe routines have settled. Maybe life feels predictable — wake up, work, dinner, laundry, bed... repeat.

And somewhere in that rhythm, you catch yourself wondering: "Is this really it?" Not because your life isn't good, but because something inside you feels like it's waiting for more.

Quiet seasons or even quiet snatches of time during the day can feel unsettling. They can make you question your purpose. Shouldn't you be doing something bigger? More? Are you missing something or falling behind?

We often see purpose as reflected in the major achievements — the awards won, the goals crushed, the recognition received. We sometimes forget our impact doesn't only show up in the big moments — it often whispers in the small ones.

In the folded laundry. In the washed dinner dishes. In the meaning behind the lights left on by kids you didn't see today. In the routines that seem ordinary but shape the people you love.

Quiet doesn't mean empty or unimportant. Quiet often means God is inviting you to pay attention.

The stillness is an opening.

It's a chance to slow down long enough to notice the things that light you up — the roles that feel meaningful and the moments where you feel most like yourself.

Purpose doesn't always shout; it often whispers
in the quiet rhythm of everyday life.

Reflect: In the quiet of your routine, where might God be nudging you toward a purpose that only you can fulfill? Where might your purpose be a whisper rather than a roar?

Polish: Identify one small action today that honors your purpose, even in routine moments.

PURPOSE SPARK 8:

LET YOUR BODY GUIDE YOU

Have you ever started talking about something and felt it in your body before you fully understood it in your mind? You get a rush or a feeling of being energized. Goosebumps. A warmth rising in your chest.

God often speaks through subtle signals long before clarity arrives in words. When your energy lifts, when time disappears, when you feel more alive while sharing or serving — that's information. Your body is responding to resonance.

Pay attention to what consistently lights you up. The topics people come to you for. The conversation that energizes you instead of draining you. The work that feels natural instead of forced. Your gifts leave a trail.

Pay just as much attention to the times when your body signals misalignment. Chronic heaviness. Tightness. Dread before something that once excited you.

It's important to listen to these cues because they can help you navigate through times of change. You may feel your purpose has stalled or is missing, but listening to your body can help you realize the dream is simply taking a new route.

When I was young, I dreamed of studying psychology and helping people. I felt that same rush then that I later felt when I discovered coaching. The path looks different now than I first imagined, but the thread is the same. The signal never left. I just had to recognize it in a new form. And my body told me everything I needed to know.

Your calling may not unfold exactly how you pictured it at 20. But when your body lights up, pay attention. When it consistently deflates, pay attention to that too.

Purpose often whispers through your physiology long before it shouts through your circumstances.

When your body reacts with a rush of excitement or energy rather than heaviness or dread, it's not random. It's a signal guiding you toward your calling and the place where your gifts are meant to serve.

Reflect: Where in your life do you feel energized, and where do you feel dread? What might those signals be trying to tell you?

Polish: Pick one way today to act on that feeling of being energized and notice what shifts when there is no dread from obligation.

THE PRESSURE HAS DONE ITS
WORK, AND NOW WHAT'S INSIDE
STARTS ASKING TO BE SEEN.

PART 2

Acceptance and Expression

This is where the coal begins to surface. The pressure has done its work, and now what's inside starts asking to be seen. In this section of Facets, you will confront the quiet beliefs that have told you that your value is conditional, that others are more qualified, more confident, more deserving. You'll examine where comparison has distorted your self-worth and learn to replace it with the truth: Your gifts are not accidental, and they are enough.

This is where the work connects with the inner and turns it outward, from self-value to expression. You'll explore what it has cost you to stay hidden and what becomes possible when you allow yourself to be seen as you truly are. This is the moment when self-acceptance meets courage, when authenticity stops feeling dangerous and starts feeling necessary. You'll stop worrying about whether the diamond will be bright enough, or too bright, and focus instead on just noticing how it catches the light.

SELF-WORTH

"You are precious in my eyes, honored, and I love you." — Isaiah 43:4

"I Look Confident, but I'm Secretly Questioning My Value"

Self-worth doubts often hide beneath competence, achievement, and a confident smile. You look strong. You look put together. You look capable. But inside, there is a quieter truth, a whisper you don't always admit:

"Am I truly enough?"

If you've achieved success yet still feel like you have something to prove, working on this Facet might help.

This proved true for Katie, a beautiful mother of five, who owns her own hair salon. She's one of those women who instantly makes others feel safe to open up to. Her warmth and empathy are natural gifts — perfectly suited for the woman behind the salon chair who is there for all the seasons of life. She's been with her customers through everyday cuts, changes in hair through the years of aging or sickness, family debates and celebrations, and more.

And yet, beneath her comforting demeanor, Katie was far from comfortable herself. Negative self-talk haunted her.

She hid behind oversized or outdated clothing. She downplayed herself out loud. "I could never wear that." "I could never do what you do."

Any time she met someone doing big things — or even small, brave things — she unconsciously removed herself from the possibility of doing anything like that herself.

And the more she spoke those doubts, the more real they became.

As she shared more of her story with me, a pattern emerged. Katie described herself as a *chameleon*. For as long as she could remember, she had always been "pretty good" at things. Good enough to fit in. Good enough to belong... but never good enough to stand out.

She was the second-oldest child in a family of five, with a sister only fifteen months older. Their parents worked hard, struggled financially, and modeled responsibility and perseverance — but they didn't encourage difference. They carried an unspoken mold designed for acceptance, and Katie learned how to adapt herself to it.

That chameleon instinct followed her into adulthood. In business, she blended in with whoever she was talking to. She mirrored their energy, their style, their confidence — because they seemed to have success she believed she hadn't earned yet. Without realizing it, she was shaping herself around other people's expectations and actions instead of her own desires. She still carried that instinct to shrink, to avoid standing out. She was avoiding being herself, as if it were something to fear.

When she and I were talking, Katie was asking, *"What should I wear?"* But underneath, what she really wanted to know was, *"How can I be taken seriously and still be myself?"*

Katie was really asking for permission to be authentic, but **the underlying problem was that she secretly didn't believe in**

her own unique value. That was why she was always adapting herself to others' expectations.

Getting her colors done created an unexpected challenge. Her color palette removed the option to blend in. She couldn't edit it. She couldn't adjust it to fit someone else's preferences. It was individual. Clear. True.

And something clicked.

For the first time in a long time, she chose something because *she loved it.* Because it worked for *her.*

That one small bit of clarity about the value of her own opinions and choices began to ripple outward into other things, such as how she approached her business and relationships. Grounded in that set of initial permissions, she gradually stopped trying to be what everyone else expected and learned to love being the person she already was.

The style process gave her back pieces of herself she realized had gone quiet in adolescence and had stayed buried through motherhood. Now, she describes it simply: *"I feel like clarity is all around me."*

And that's the key.

Self-doubt never vanishes, and it didn't for her. But now, she recognizes it faster. She doesn't stay stuck there. She has awareness. She has tools. She can feel when she is honoring her own true value compared to when she's trying to adapt and look like someone else to achieve acceptance. She recognizes when her self-perception is giving her false messages that she's not worthy, and she knows how to counter them.

Those false messages are tricky. They can even shape themselves around your success, which is what happened to me.

Somewhere between building a brand, running my home, and being everything to everyone, I started tying my worth to my performance. Others' applause felt validating, but the silence afterward felt empty. I believed my value lived in my output, not in my existence. My output became the topic of my "not enough" beliefs. And yet, that was an untrue message — a self-judgment based on unrealistic expectations I hadn't questioned.

Your True Value Is Immeasurable

The truth is, talking yourself down only brings you down. What you say becomes true if your subconscious hears it. When you set unrealistic expectations, you're bound to fail to meet them.

Are you in this negative state of mind? Most of us have been at one time or another. We doubt ourselves. We look for some kind of external validation, but we never accept it when we receive it.

WHAT NEGATIVE SELF-WORTH LOOKS LIKE

Here's what happens when you're fighting this kind of battle against yourself:

- You downplay your abilities, even when others see your strengths.
- You speak doubt out loud before anyone else can.
- You hide behind comparison or self-critical humor.
- You feel capable in some areas but invisible in others.
- You struggle to see yourself as others experience you.
- You shrink your self-expression to avoid standing out or failing.

What Polishing This Facet Will Bring

Working on this Facet will help you reshape your self-view. You will:

- Use self-talk to shape your reality positively, not negatively.
- Recognize when your perspective is distorted by fear or comparison.
- Feel comfortable as you truly are — capable, gifted, whole.
- Value your authentic gifts and knowledge rather than unrealistic ideas of perfection.
- Show up even when insecurity whispers.

Over time, you'll realize you're now looking at yourself with compassion instead of criticism, curiosity instead of judgment. You'll feel confidence rooted in awareness, not in the need to prove. You'll have freedom to express yourself without overexplaining. You'll still have doubts, but they won't get to lead.

How We'll Get There

The next eight Sparks of Wisdom will help you reconnect with your own value and stop the habits that are undermining you. You'll learn to:

- Separate who you are from the stories you've told yourself.
- Identify where your self-image has been shaped by fear or comparison.
- Interrupt the habit of speaking doubt into existence.
- Reframe insecurity without shaming yourself for it.
- Practice seeing yourself with clarity instead of distortion.
- Build trust in who you are becoming.
- Show up authentically, even when confidence feels shaky.

Your worth has never been in question. It has simply been cloaked in an illusion woven by years of belief in unrealistic self-expectations and untrue self-perceptions.

This is where you finally reclaim it.

A diamond doesn't lose value because of the way it's viewed. But the way it's seen determines how it's handled, set, and appreciated. Under the wrong light, its brilliance can be missed. Viewed through distortion, its beauty can be overlooked. Yet only the perspective changes, not the diamond or its worth.

Your true value has never been in question, no matter how much your negative self-perception has been muting its shine. You don't need to become more to be enough. You just need to see yourself clearly and allow that revelation to lead.

REWRITE THE INNER SCRIPT

Sometimes it doesn't matter how many compliments you receive or how proud you feel of your accomplishments; one critical comment can stop you in your tracks. And years of criticism, whether from others or the voice in your own head, can dig deeply, creating doubts that are hard to shake.

That critical voice can make you question your abilities, your decisions, and even your worth as a person. As we saw with Katie's story in the Facet introduction, that doubt can deactivate your confidence in a way that keeps you from stepping into the life you were made to live.

What if this judgmental voice belongs to someone you deeply care about — a parent, a spouse, or a mentor? When you love and respect them, their words can echo even more loudly in your mind and hold you back, leaving you feeling stuck or "not enough."

Remember: Their opinion does *not* define you unless you allow it to. Your value does not depend on someone else's perception. You are made for more, and you can reclaim your confidence, one step at a time, simply by choosing to view yourself differently.

So, when you start noticing the moment your body tightens after a comment, or you keep replaying their words in your head and catching yourself mid-spiral, or even when the tears want to start rolling... pause. Instead of immediately assuming they're right, try to ask yourself, "Is this truth, or is this the other person's lens?"

We rarely know the full story behind someone else's judgment. A husband may sound critical, when underneath, he's really afraid your growth means he'll lose you. A mentor may use language shaped by their own experiences, not yours. A parent may project their own unresolved disappointments onto your ambition. And sometimes, what lands as criticism was clumsy encouragement filtered through insecurity.

Growth doesn't mean you stop caring about what people think. It means you stop letting their fear define your self-worth.

Someone else's opinion is not your meter to rate your worth.
Replace the critic's echo with the truth of who God says you are.

 **Reflect:** Which critical voices — internal or external — have influenced the way you see yourself? How have they shaped your choices? Which beliefs about yourself are *not* true?

 **Polish:** Today, identify one thought or comment that has held you back, and replace it with a new realization about yourself. Write it down, say it aloud, or post it somewhere visible. Example: "I am capable. I am enough. I am worthy of pursuing my dreams." Repeat it whenever doubt creeps in and notice how reclaiming your voice changes your day.

DROP THE BODY CRITIC AND EMBRACE YOUR GRACE

I remember high school, staring in the dressing-room mirror, feeling like I had the ugliest body, the smallest chest, and that I could never compare to the other girls. Fast forward to today — I look at those old pictures and wish I had appreciated my body then!

And yet, though many of us can see how untrue our negative impressions of ourselves were in the past, we still carry the same kinds of insecurities.

Let's not wait until some future date to start questioning what's real.

Think about everything your body has carried you through —children, hard work, challenges, accidents, age, and perhaps the changes of perimenopause if you've reached that season in your life. We know we could make lifestyle adjustments in diet or exercise, yet so often, we continue "living life" while silently beating ourselves up over our appearance.

We hide from photos, make everyone promise not to post or share, or tear ourselves apart while quietly comparing ourselves to the world around us.

And yet, we would never, *ever*, speak to our daughters, friends, or loved ones the harsh words we speak to ourselves. I can just imagine the way that scenario would play out if I heard someone talk to my daughter that way. Mama Bear would be in full force, and it would be like the movie where you see yourself attacking someone and ripping their hair out or a nice throat punch...

... before you snap out of it and realize you were daydreaming!

Why, then, do we allow *ourselves* this self-cruelty?

It's time to treat ourselves with the same love, grace, and kindness we extend to others. Our bodies are amazing; they are resilient, capable, and worthy of respect and celebration. Let's focus on gratitude for what we have instead of criticism for what we aren't. Our future selves will agree with us.

You would never speak to someone you love the way you speak to yourself. Your body deserves the same grace, gratitude, and kindness you give everyone else.

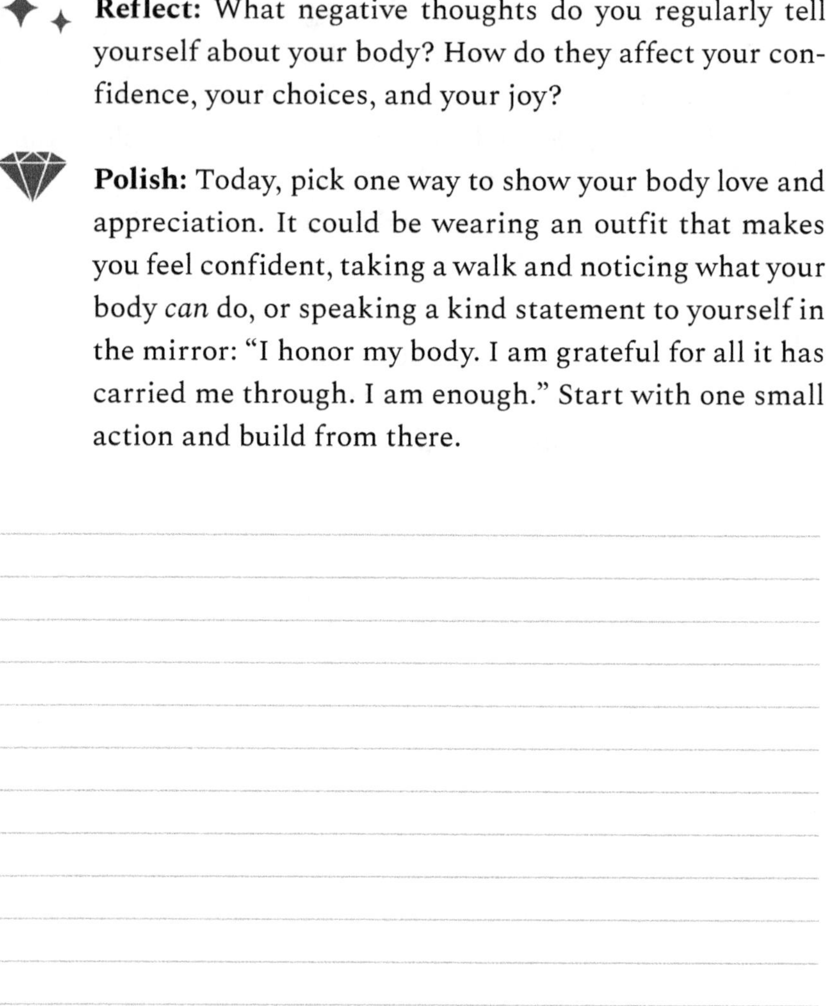

Reflect: What negative thoughts do you regularly tell yourself about your body? How do they affect your confidence, your choices, and your joy?

Polish: Today, pick one way to show your body love and appreciation. It could be wearing an outfit that makes you feel confident, taking a walk and noticing what your body *can* do, or speaking a kind statement to yourself in the mirror: "I honor my body. I am grateful for all it has carried me through. I am enough." Start with one small action and build from there.

SELF-WORTH SPARK 3:

LET GO OF THE ILLUSION AND RECOGNIZE THE REALITY UNDERNEATH

How many hours each day or week do we spend comparing ourselves to others? On social media or in social situations, we see smiling faces, perfect complexions, and gleaming new cars or gushing descriptions of perfect vacations. We spiral, thinking, *"They got lucky,"* or *"Why not me?"* We question why opportunities, money, or recognition seem to land in someone else's lap.

But do we really know what's behind the happy faces and perfect presentation? Are they secretly living paycheck to paycheck? Struggling with loss or debt? Hiding tears under the smile or wrinkles and blemishes under filters? Are they playing the same comparison game you are, and never feeling like they measure up either? Maybe she has perfect curls or a naturally thin frame, but she probably wishes she could change something about herself too.

God created each of us unique, with our own gifts, beauty, and purpose. Your life, your body, your talents — they are perfect for you. Instead of comparing, embrace what is yours. Someone, somewhere, is wishing they had your strength, your skills, or your experiences.

Comparison steals your confidence. What God designed for you will never be found in someone else's highlight reel.

Reflect: What areas of your life do you find yourself comparing to others? How does it make you feel about yourself and your worth?

Polish: Today, choose one thing about yourself, your life, or your accomplishments to celebrate. Write it down, say it out loud, or share it with someone who will cheer for you. Let this small act of self-acknowledgment remind you that your journey is yours alone, and it's enough.

HEAL THE ROOT TRIGGER AND BREAK FREE FROM YOUR PAST

It took me years of soul-searching to uncover the roots of my inner struggles and understand why certain situations trigger me, why some thoughts create anxiety in my gut, and why I sometimes doubt myself.

Sometimes it feels easier to bury old wounds or to sweep difficult experiences under the rug. And yes, there are times when leaving some stones unturned is wiser. But when we do open that can of worms, we can take a deep, honest look at our story and see it as a God-given life lesson. Every painful moment, every struggle shaped who you are today. And in that understanding, you can choose to grow stronger, wiser, and more resilient.

Old wounds can fester if you let them define you, but when you choose to confront the lies, to rewrite the narrative, and to be the hero of your own story, those scars transform into power.

Your past doesn't define you — it prepares you.
When you face the old wounds, they lose their power
and become the source of your strength.

Reflect: What old wound or past experience still influences how you see yourself? How might seeing it as a lesson rather than a limitation change your perspective?

Polish: Choose one small way to honor your growth from that past experience. Write a letter to your younger self, journal your feelings, or simply speak an affirming truth to yourself today. Begin reclaiming your power over the story you tell about yourself.

CHOOSE THE EMPOWERING LESSON OVER THE DIMINISHING ONE

When God places an idea on your heart, do you feel an instant response — momentum, clarity, excitement? Are there times when you maybe move forward faster than wisdom intended, ignoring the gentle nudge to pause, pray, or prepare? When things don't turn out the way you hoped, it's easy to label the experience as failure or assume it reflects your worth, your talent, or your likability.

But what if you choose to see it another way?

Every misstep carries information. You can choose to fill it with condemnation or not. The lesson reveals what you're passionate about, what you're gifted at, what needs refining, and what supports your growth.

Instead of assuming you "missed it," consider that you might have been gathering wisdom, resilience, or clarity, which you'll need for the next opportunity.

Sometimes the experience is teaching you a lesson about better timing. Or perhaps it is teaching you to adjust your direction. Sometimes the lesson is one of trust.

The experience doesn't have to teach you that you're a failure because something didn't work out the first time. You are simply practicing your skills and evaluating where to improve. Each lesson shapes, strengthens, and refines you so that when the door opens again, you can step through it with greater wisdom, confidence, and faith.

Redeem the lesson. Don't waste it beating yourself up.

Failure isn't proof you missed your calling — sometimes it's proof God is preparing you for it. The timing of achieving your purpose is just as important as the purpose itself.

Reflect: Where have you labeled something a failure when it was really a valuable lesson in disguise? How has your fear of failure held you back from trusting your instincts or following your purpose?

Polish: Identify one past experience that felt like a failure. Write down the lesson you learned and one way it prepared you for the next chapter of your life. Carry that lesson forward today, and apply it to a current decision or opportunity.

SEE SCARS AS MARKS OF HEALING

Packing for a beach vacation always starts the same way... trying on swimsuits. Every woman's favorite confidence test.

I throw in the one-piece (because it feels safer) and pack a bikini *just in case*. Every time, I kick myself when I get there because it's hot, I'm uncomfortable, and every other woman on the beach seems to be living her best bikini life.

I used to look at those women — flawless tans, no cellulite, flat stomachs — and think, *I wish*. But then I'd look at my body.

Three C-sections.

Three babies delivered.

Three miracles scarred into my skin.

My stomach doesn't look the same as it once did, and yet, neither do I. *On the inside.*

That scar is part of my story. And our stories are vital. Women don't bond over perfection. We bond over the stories behind our scars.

When I stopped seeing my scar as a flaw and started seeing it as a symbol, it became less about what my body looks like — and more about what my body *has done*.

You don't have to love every mark on your body to honor the story it tells.

Whatever scar you carry — visible or invisible — it's not shameful. It's proof you survived.

Your scar is not a flaw — it's evidence of your strength.
Don't hide the story that shaped you.

Reflect: What part of your body have you criticized that actually represents a moment of bravery, growth, or love?

Polish: Find one scar, stretch mark, or "flaw," place your hand over it, and say out loud:

"Thank you. You are proof of what I've lived through."

Now, write one sentence about the story that scar represents.

REMOVE "JUST A..." FROM YOUR VOCABULARY

I remember standing in the preschool hallway one morning, coffee in hand, listening to another mom introduce herself with a nervous laugh: "I'm just a mom." Those three little words sank into me.

Just a mom. Somewhere along the way, the world had convinced her that raising tiny humans, managing a home, and shaping the next generation wasn't important.

Some of us are made to be working moms; others are called to be stay-at-home moms. Neither is right or wrong — it's simply what fits the life God designed for each of us. Ironically, those of us who aren't made to be stay-at-home moms can wrestle with just as much self-doubt, but it comes in the form of guilt. Perhaps you've heard the quiet comments about "working too much" or "letting someone else raise the kids."

Is that really fair? Did you ever miss the moments that mattered? I know I didn't! I was there for the field trips, the lunchroom shifts, the school pick-ups, and the bedtime routines. And I made sure my kids had great care when I wasn't there. My grandma lovingly cared for them while I built our business alongside my husband, Mark. My children didn't grow up lacking love; they grew up watching their mom live her calling.

Motherhood doesn't look the same for everyone. Believing you're "just a mom" is accepting a lie designed to make women question their worth. And so is feeling guilty for wanting a career.

Whether you work full-time, part-time, or spend your days keeping the home running, you are doing sacred work. You are shaping hearts, showing strength, and leading by example. You are never *just* anything. You are *exactly* where God wants you to be.

Motherhood doesn't come with a label. Your worth isn't measured by hours, but by love, presence in the moment, and intention.

 **Reflect:** Where in your life have you said or thought, *"I'm just a..."*? What label have you used to minimize the sacred work you're already doing?

 **Polish:** Rewrite that sentence today. Instead of "I'm just a mom," try "I am a mom, and I am building a family rooted in love and purpose." If you are talking about yourself as "just a" in reference to something else, use the same kind of language, focusing on its importance. Write it on a sticky note and place it where you'll see it every morning. Let it remind you that "just a..." doesn't belong in your vocabulary anymore.

YOU'RE A PROBLEM-SOLVER, NOT A BURDEN

Have you ever caught yourself texting someone and suddenly every message is wrapped in an apology?

"I'm sorry to bother you..." "I'm sorry, I have a question..." "I'm sorry it's so late..." "I'm sorry it's so early..."

You hit *send* and instantly wonder if you sounded annoying, needy, or inconvenient — so you scroll back through the thread and count the apologies. And the pattern becomes clear: it's not that you're doing something wrong; it's that you don't believe what you have to say is important.

I see this often with my own clients. I tell them over and over, *"You're not bothering me. If you need help, ask — that's what I'm here for."*

And yet later, they'll admit they still hesitated.

They didn't want to be a burden.

They didn't want to need too much.

They didn't want to take up my time.

People-pleasing shows up not only in how we apologize, but in who we apologize *to*. We minimize our needs with the people we value most because, deep down, we doubt our worthiness of their time, attention, or guidance.

If you hired a coach, mentor, or professional, you are not interrupting them by using the service you invested in. You are honoring the agreement. If a friend says, "Call me anytime," and you never do because you're afraid of being inconvenient, you are quietly deciding their generosity wasn't real.

You are not a burden. Your questions are valid. Your presence isn't an interruption — it's a connection.

You don't need to apologize for needing help or taking up space. Your voice matters, your questions matter, and you are never a burden to those who are meant to support you.

Reflect: Who are the people you find yourself apologizing to the most — and what does that reveal about how you value yourself in that relationship?

Polish: Send one message this week *without* softening it with "sorry." Ask the question, share the thought, or make the request with confidence — and notice how empowering it feels to speak without shrinking.

AUTHENTICITY

"Let your light shine before others, so that they may see your good works and give glory to your Father in heaven." — Matthew 5:16

**"I want to show the real me,
but what if others judge me?**

When women aren't living their authentic lives, fear of judgment is often the underlying reason. It can be subtle. It sounds protective and logical: "Stay small, stay safe." "Don't make waves." "Who are you to want more?"

Unfortunately, this fear identifies your true self as a threat — something you need protection from. And so, it keeps you from being who you really are.

This Facet might seem similar to Self-Worth, yet they are not quite the same. The Self-Worth Facet revolves around how you see and value your own worth, while Authenticity focuses on how your decisions and actions reflect your true values and priorities. Are you really being true to yourself, or are you playing it safe to avoid others' judgment?

Every time I think of this Facet, I think of Shelby. She came to me bursting with excitement about a new business idea. She was clear and confident in her purpose and deeply passionate about the impact her product could make.

On paper, she had everything she needed to make it happen. She looked like a superstar. Along with starting her business, she was writing a chapter in a book. Exploring new leadership roles. Considering hiring clients. Navigating a parenting approach that looked very different from the family systems she grew up with and from the ones around her. In a variety of ways, she was stretching herself far outside her comfort zone.

Seeing her passion for her business, I was excited for her, too. And yet, I couldn't help noticing that her appearance and the way she carried herself didn't reflect her smart, ambitious nature. She held herself in a timid, slouching posture as if she were trying not to capture attention. She wore baggy clothes and no makeup. Her hair was pulled back in a hastily arranged ponytail. She seemed to be trying to hide, as if hesitant to put herself and her ideas forward.

Her manner didn't imply confidence, and I'm sure others felt that way, too. After a failed pitch of her idea to a storefront, Shelby realized something was wrong and started looking into what was going on.

She admitted that her timid approach wasn't doing her product justice. After looking more deeply, she realized why she felt so hesitant.

The more she pushed out of her comfort zone, the more her insecurities were triggered. Though she was excited about her business idea, underneath she worried that she wasn't skilled enough to achieve it. Meanwhile, the new parenting strategies had brought unexpected and unwanted scrutiny from others. In the midst of all of these things, old wounds surfaced — childhood patterns, critical inner voices, and a longing for appreciation and approval she hadn't always received.

While she did partly struggle to believe in herself — an issue of self-worth — her main struggle was her fear of others' judgment. What if they disapproved? What if they didn't like who she really was? What if they judged her as a failure?

Shelby knew something had to change, and it had to be her. Her goals were important and would help others. To succeed, her business needed her to be visible. Her leadership needed to be felt and acknowledged. She needed confidence even in the face of judgment. She couldn't lead boldly while hiding.

With this understanding, Shelby challenged herself to stop listening to the doubts and fears and to instead ground herself in her own decisions again. She worked to express this commitment not only through her style decisions, but also through how she stood, moved, spoke, and handled judgment.

As she worked through the challenges, she began to feel grounded in her body again. Strong. Unapologetic. *Badass*, as she put it.

Grounding in her own values and personal style gave her permission to be seen, to move forward without apologizing. She had re-empowered herself simply by reconnecting with herself.

With her renewed inner power, she also began to recognize the difference between worry and intuition. Worry tended to spiral into chaos, but intuition showed up as a steady feeling — a knowing that kept returning. She practiced trusting and following that knowing instead of reasoning herself out of decisions. She stopped waiting for validation and started leading from alignment.

RECLAIM THE POWER OF BEING YOU

If you see yourself in Shelby — confident in your ideas but hesitant to step fully into them — you're not alone. For many women, the struggle isn't from lack of purpose or capability; it's the idea that their validity should come from somewhere outside themselves.

What Authenticity Struggles Look Like

Working in this Facet may help you if you are any of the following:

- Afraid to take up space or let your presence be fully felt.
- Confident in your ideas, but hesitant to be the face of them.
- Worried that others won't take you seriously if you're fully seen.
- Torn between your inner authority and a different outer version of you that feels safe.
- Pulled toward leadership, but uncomfortable with visibility.
- Tempted to soften, minimize, or over-explain to avoid judgment.

What Polishing the Authenticity Facet Will Bring You

Working on this Facet will help you:

- Allow your outer presence to reflect your inner confidence.
- Own your gifts without apologizing or over-explaining.
- Show up as the credible, capable woman you already are.
- Lead with your unique expression of your gifts instead of merely trying to meet empty, trendy goals, such as "being more efficient."

- Trust God's calling more than others' comfort.
- Feel safe being seen, known, and respected.

You'll find the courage to replace hesitation, self-editing, and apology, and you'll stand behind your work instead of shrinking from it.

How We'll Get There

The next eight Sparks of Wisdom will help you:

- Identify where you've learned to stay small to feel safe.
- Release the belief that credibility comes only from approval.
- Align your inner gifts and authority with your outer presence.
- Let God's voice be louder than judgment or doubt.
- Embrace visibility as stewardship, not self-promotion.

Authenticity doesn't guarantee you'll never feel insecure or be judged. You simply learn to find peace in choosing to be you instead of succumbing to pressure.

Inclusions don't weaken a diamond; they make it unmistakably unique. When the diamond remains hidden for fear of how people will judge these qualities, its brilliance cannot be recognized.

Your doubts, history, and humanity don't diminish you. They tell your story. Your uniqueness is meant to be seen, not tucked away. It is why others will want to connect with you. When others can clearly see the vision and purpose you were entrusted to carry, they will be more likely to want to help achieve it.

SHOW UP AS YOU ARE

We probably all know someone we admire — a beautiful, relaxed woman who lights up any room she walks into. She's the one whose laugh carries, whose presence lifts the whole group, whose energy makes everything more fun.

And we've probably also noticed another woman who *could* be like that — but her laugh is a little too polite, her smile is a bit too fixed, and her manner is just slightly too careful... because secretly, she is terrified of how she'll be perceived.

Which one describes you?

Authenticity isn't just about how you look; it's also about whether the woman who shows up with strangers resembles the woman who feels free at home. It's about whether your personality shrinks when the room changes.

Realizing that, think how distorted our self-image can become, simply by worrying about judgment. We always want what we don't have: curly hair wants straight; tall wants average; athletic wants slim. We forget that God made each of us in His image — *and made us uniquely beautiful.* One size does not fit all, in clothes or in life.

I'm still a work in progress too. But every time I give myself a bad review, I remember that my daughter — at 21 years old — is still watching me. She's learning how to see herself by watching how I treat myself. And I want her to learn confidence, not fear of visibility, from me.

When you're busy scanning the room for approval, you can't fully connect with the people in it. When you're filtering every sentence before it leaves your mouth, you miss the spontaneous laughter, the honest disagreement, the deeper questions that create real intimacy.

When you're trying to be impressive, agreeable, or safe, you don't get to be known.

You lose the chance for someone to say, "Me too." You lose the opportunity for your honesty to unlock theirs. You lose the kind of connection that only happens when masks come off.

You are far more beautiful than your insecurities
let you believe. Don't hide from the camera —
your presence is worth remembering.

Reflect: When was the last time you avoided being in a photo, and what fear or belief was behind that moment?

Polish: Take one photo today — unedited, unfiltered — and keep it. You don't have to post it. Just look at it with softer eyes and speak one kind affirmation about the woman you see.

DARE TO BE UNFILTERED

Working in a world built on Facebook, Instagram, and endless scrolling, it's easy to look at everyone else's "perfect life" and wonder where you went wrong. But if we're honest, most of us know exactly what's behind those posts — angles, retakes, filters, drafts, and perfectly curated moments that hide the mess just outside the frame.

How many times have you taken 20 versions of the same picture, trying to get the right lighting... only to delete all of them? How many posts sit in your drafts because you're afraid of what people will think? How many thoughts, celebrations, or stories have you swallowed because visibility felt too risky?

I've been there too. But over time, we can learn something powerful: *Our flaws, the real stories, the unfiltered moments — that's where connection lives.*

These days, I take one or two pictures and post them. I create a reel in five minutes and hit publish. Not because I'm perfect or brave every day, but because I refuse to let fear silence the message God gave me. In a world drowning in filters, stolen content, and "aesthetic feeds," authenticity stands out like a diamond in the rough.

You're not meant to be perfect. You're meant to be **visible**.

Somewhere, someone needs what you're sharing — exactly as you are.

Your drafts don't serve anyone. Your real, imperfect voice does.
You weren't made to be flawless — you were made to be seen.

Reflect: What post, picture, or idea have you kept in your drafts out of fear — and what story would it tell if you shared it bravely?

Polish: Choose one draft, photo, or message you've hesitated to share. Either post it today or rewrite it in a way that feels authentic to you and post it tomorrow. Let it be imperfect — and let it be enough.

OWN YOUR STORY

I've met countless women with stories that could move mountains — stories of transformation after years of pain, trauma, illness, betrayal, or heartache. But when it comes time to speak those stories out loud, they shrink.

Why? Because they're afraid — afraid of exposing the truth that shaped them. Afraid of judgment, of losing friendships, of being misunderstood. Afraid that sharing their story might cost them more than it gives.

But their reality is the very thing that made them who they are now. And it's often the very thing that someone else desperately needs to hear.

We can also forget that sharing our story isn't about reliving trauma — it's about releasing it. Stories can heal us even while giving someone else permission to believe they aren't alone, broken, or beyond redemption.

I truly believe God gives us these experiences — and carries us through them — not to shame us, but to empower us to help others. Sometimes, sharing is the test of faith itself.

It reminds me of the Biblical account of Job. He lost everything. He grieved. He questioned. He wrestled. But he never cursed God. He stayed faithful, and God restored him twofold. Job's suffering wasn't the end of his story; it was the testimony that revealed God's glory.

So, if you're tempted to shrink, to hide your story, or to protect others from the weight of your certainty... **don't.** Your story is not a burden. It is a bridge.

And God will stand with you as you speak it.

Your story isn't meant to shame you — it's meant to free you. When you resist shrinking, you step into the purpose God built from your pain. Someone's healing is waiting for your courage.

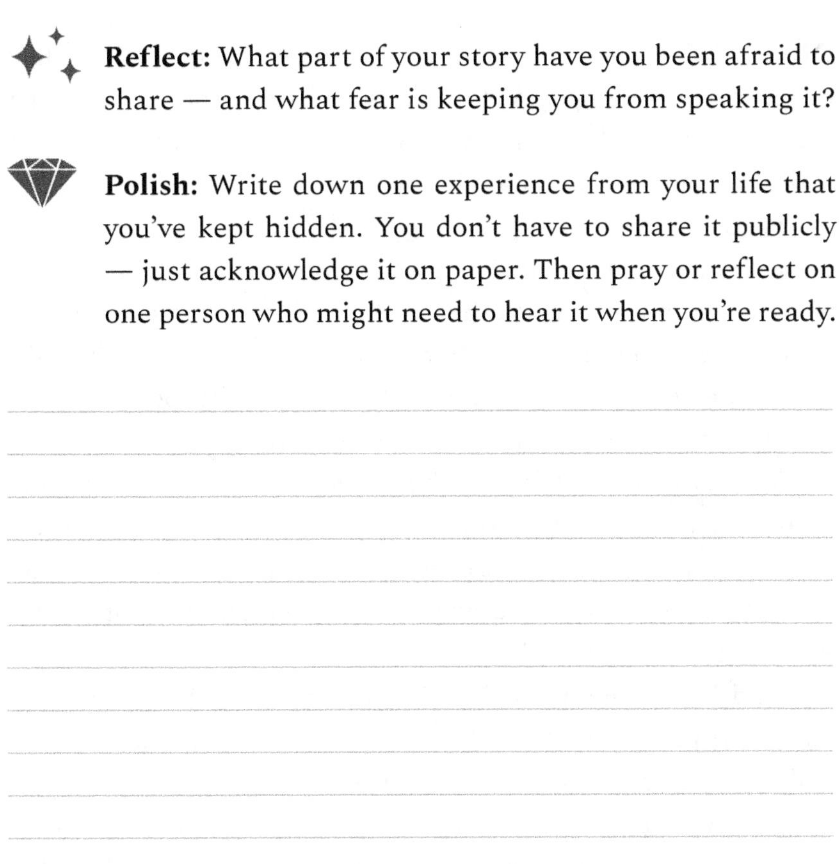

Reflect: What part of your story have you been afraid to share — and what fear is keeping you from speaking it?

Polish: Write down one experience from your life that you've kept hidden. You don't have to share it publicly — just acknowledge it on paper. Then pray or reflect on one person who might need to hear it when you're ready.

ASK FOR CONFIDENCE

Oh, how I *wish* I could sing — and sound good! I still belt it out in church, but my kids' side glances tell the whole story. (Remember how badly I want to play guitar? Well, singing is right up there on the dream list too!)

So, the first time I heard my super-shy friend Lily sing late one night, I practically stopped breathing. Our small group of friends was tucked in a room together in the back of a karaoke bar. We were relaxed and laughing after a few glasses of wine when she belted out "Baby Got Back" for the few of us in the room.

Her voice was stunning — soft but strong, full of emotion, the kind of voice that makes the whole room feel still. I immediately asked her why she didn't sing on stage or during church.

Her answer? With wide eyes, she whispered, "I would rather die than sing in front of anyone but my daughter. I don't want everyone staring at me."

And in that moment, I realized something: So many of us have God-given talents we keep hidden — not because we lack ability, but because we fear being seen.

Somewhere along the way, someone's comment, someone's judgment, or our own inner criticism convinced us to dim what God designed to shine.

If God gave you the gift, He can give you the confidence to use it. All you have to do is ask.

I continue to pray that one day my sweet friend Lily will share her voice with the world. And I hope you pray the same for the gift inside *you*. Because someone, somewhere, is waiting to be blessed by it.

You don't hide your gifts because you lack talent — you hide them because visibility feels vulnerable. If God gave you the gift, He can strengthen your confidence to carry it.

Reflect: What ability or desire have you kept private because being seen feels riskier than staying hidden?

Polish: Ask God for boldness in one specific area this week — then take one small, visible step that lets your gift be seen.

AUTHENTICITY SPARK 5:

VOICE YOUR PREFERENCE

Have you ever been in a group text trying to make plans and every single person says, "I don't care, whatever works"?

No one wants to be the one who chooses. No one wants to be the one who inconveniences. It seems silly, doesn't it? But so many of us are guilty of it. Unless you're a high-yang personality — the type who knows exactly what she wants and says it boldly — you're probably like the rest of us. We tend to go with the flow, choosing whatever keeps the peace, even when it's not what we actually want.

I once saw a restaurant named "I Don't Care, You Decide" and laughed because... honestly? Genius. They built an entire brand around the very thing women say every day.

But when we can't speak up about what we want for dinner, it often reflects something bigger happening in our lives. Maybe we don't want to inconvenience anyone. Maybe we're afraid of being judged as "picky" or "difficult." Maybe we've gotten so used to people-pleasing that we've lost touch with what we genuinely want.

This type of authenticity issue is not so much about dinner as it is about honoring your desires — even the small ones. Believe it or not, practicing confidence in the small decisions builds courage for the big ones.

How about Mexican food tonight? (You're thinking about tacos and margaritas now, aren't you!)

When you silence your preferences to keep the peace, you teach yourself that your voice doesn't matter. Even the smallest preference — like where to eat — is a chance to practice choosing yourself.

Reflect: Where in your life do you minimize your preferences to avoid conflict, and what fear lies underneath that silence?

Polish: Today, name one preference out loud — where to eat, what movie to watch, what route to take, anything. Practice choosing, even in the small things, so your confidence grows for the big things.

ANCHOR YOURSELF IN GOD'S APPROVAL

For years, I chased approval — from my mom, my peers, my spouse, even my children. As someone whose love language is words of affirmation, I longed to hear the praise, the validation, the "I'm proud of you." But when I did hear it, I couldn't receive it. I believed people said it out of obligation, not truth. I still felt like I wasn't enough to please them — like something in me was always missing.

One day, I woke up and realized: *If I'm living for their approval, I can't fully live for God.* And that reality set me free to sparkle unapologetically.

It took years of coaching, deep self-reflection, solo retreats, and countless prayers to finally see the truth: **I was enough the whole time.** The Holy Spirit had been carrying me through every season of doubt, every wound, every misunderstanding that shaped the way I saw myself.

Yes — people said things that hurt. Yes — I have evidence to support why I doubted myself. But I also have faith strong enough to understand that none of it was meant to break me. And none of it was meant to define me.

For so long, I apologized for who I was, for needing too much, for being too much — or not enough.

But now I know: *The apology I needed most was the one I owed myself.*

If this sounds familiar: Forgive yourself. Release the old narratives. And stand in awe of who you really are.

When you stop living for their approval, you finally make space to live fully for God. The moment you release your focus on people-pleasing, your true light begins to shine — unapologetically and beautifully.

Reflect: Where in your life are you still seeking approval — and how might your heart change if you begin seeking God's affirmation instead?

Polish: Write down three ways you know you are already "enough," not because someone told you, but because God made you that way. Let this become your new truth statement for the week.

YOUR PEOPLE NEED THE REAL YOU

You are meant to attract your people. But that only happens when they can recognize you.

I have a friend, Rachel, who carefully curated everything she shared online. Perfect lighting. Perfect captions. Perfect angles. It looked polished and professional, and she was proud of it.

But she kept saying the same thing: "I don't know why I'm not attracting the women I actually want to work with."

When we peeled it back, we realized that, while it looked impressive, it didn't sound like her.

In real life, she was witty. Direct. A little sarcastic. Deeply thoughtful. She asked bold questions in conversation. But online? She was neutral. Safe. Generic. She was trying to sound like what she thought a "successful influencer" should sound like.

When she finally posted something raw and simple — no graphics, no fluff — just a story about a recent struggle and what she learned from it, her inbox changed overnight. Not because it went viral, but because the right women saw themselves in it.

They said things like, "I thought I was the only one." "I've never heard someone say it like that." "This feels like me."

That's what authenticity does. It filters out the crowd and draws in connection. **Fake perfection may attract attention, but authenticity attracts alignment.**

Without authenticity, you miss the deeper conversations. You miss the women who would have felt safe with you. You miss the partnerships, friendships, and opportunities that require the real version of you to exist.

So, go ahead...

Post the thought before it's perfectly packaged.

Speak up in the room instead of rehearsing silently.

Admit what you believe instead of scanning for approval first.

If you stay in the safe, polished version of yourself, you may still succeed. But you'll build that success around a filtered identity — one that's hard to maintain. Your people are not looking for the most impressive woman in the room. They're looking for the most honest one.

Authenticity attracts the people meant for you.
You don't need to perform like anyone else — God will send
your message to the women who need your voice.

Reflect: Where in your life are you polishing your image instead of expressing your truth — and what kind of connection might you be missing because of it?

Polish: Create one simple piece of content today — no trends, no pressure — just your heart, your voice, your message. Practice showing up as *you*, not the person you think you're supposed to be.

LET THEM ADJUST

I recently ran into a childhood friend at the store. She looked at me and said, "I can't believe the Nicole I knew is who you are today."

She didn't mean it unkindly. We grew up in similar circumstances. And unspoken in her words was a truth many women quietly carry — the expectation that we stay small, familiar, and unchanged.

Why? Because sometimes our growth can feel threatening to others. Especially those who know you best. They were comfortable with the old version of you. The version that was easier to predict. Easier to explain. Easier to keep in the same familiar routines.

And then, you begin to grow and change. Your voice sounds steadier than it used to. Your faith deepens. Your alignment crystallizes and achieves clarity.

Suddenly, the people who love you most start wondering how your growth will impact *them*. Spouses are often the first to voice these kinds of concerns. They fear their partner will eventually outgrow them.

In those situations, authenticity requires a different kind of courage. Can you, despite others' fears, honor who you are becoming?

It is your responsibility to steward the gifts and values God placed in you. Don't let others' fear or judgment decide how brightly you're allowed to live.

You are not responsible for making your evolution comfortable for others. You don't need to over-explain your growth. You don't need to perform as the old version of yourself to preserve peace. And, you don't need permission to become more aligned, more joyful, more you.

You also don't have to accept the situation as growing *away* from others. It just means you're growing into yourself. You're becoming more grounded, more whole, and more present.

This version of you is better for them, not further from them.

When you choose to align with the real you, some people will need time to adjust. Let them remember the old you if they need to, but don't let that memory keep you from honoring the woman you are becoming.

You don't need to make your growth comfortable for the people who remember an older version of you. When you choose self-alignment over approval, others may need time to adjust — and that's fine. It doesn't mean you're wrong; it's just a part of being real.

Reflect: Where are you still editing yourself around people who know you well — and what are you afraid would change if you fully lived in alignment?

Polish: Notice one moment this week when you're tempted to shrink, soften, or explain yourself unnecessarily. Pause. Breathe. And choose to stay rooted in who you are now.

THE DIAMOND IS NO LONGER
FRAGILE OR TENTATIVE, THOUGH
IT'S STILL BEING REFINED AND
CUT TO ENHANCE ITS CLARITY.

PART 3

Decisions, Priorities, and Connections

This is where the diamond is fully exposed to and directing the light. It's no longer fragile or tentative, though it's still being refined and cut to enhance its clarity. In this section, the work shifts from knowing and accepting yourself to *acting* as the woman you already are, achieving your unique mission.

You will examine how much permission you've been waiting for before making decisions and learn to root decisiveness in your own gifts instead of borrowed certainty or endless overthinking. Action becomes a place of experimentation rather than proof.

From there, you will bring intention to your focus, changing from doing more to choosing better. You'll learn to clear out the lingering "shoulds," outdated roles, and people-pleasing habits that have been scattering your energy, and you'll align instead with your purpose in this season.

Finally, because no diamond achieves its best shine in isolation, this section also addresses how you can make the most of all your connections. You'll look honestly at the relationships that drain you and the ones that strengthen you, and you'll claim the right to cultivate a circle that supports who you are becoming. These are the polishing strokes that happen through movement, boundaries, and brave choices made in real life.

DECISIVENESS

Let your light shine before others, so that they may see your good works and give glory to your Father in heaven. — Matthew 5:16

**"I want to move forward,
but I keep second-guessing myself."**

Decision paralysis is not a lack of desire. It's rooted in the tension between who you are now and who you're being called to become.

On the outside, it can look like "being thoughtful," "weighing options," or "waiting for the right moment." But inside, it feels like fear and worry:

"What if I make the wrong choice?"

"What if it fails?"

"What if I'm not skilled/knowledgeable/strong/etc. enough?"

In this mindset, every decision feels dangerous. Unfortunately, many women are taught to think this way early in their lives. That is what happened with Leisa, another of my clients.

In the household where she grew up, people made choices based on obedience and consequence, not guided by instinct or trust. Women submitted. Decisions were made based on what was "right," not what was felt. And "wrong" choices often brought unwanted repercussions.

Navigating this landscape, Leisa learned to be careful. As an adult, that carefulness showed up as overthinking. Researching. Weighing every option. Googling to make sure she had all the information before committing.

Her actions looked responsible — even wise. Yet the constant self-scrutiny exhausted her. Even simple choices like where to eat, whether to go out with friends, or whether to spend five dollars felt heavy. Worst-case scenarios tumbled through her mind, creating unnecessary stress before she ever gave a decision a chance.

After finally deciding, she'd wake up at night in a panic — replaying the choice, wondering how to undo it, afraid she'd made a mistake.

Over time, the inner pressure caused her to isolate herself from others. Invitations sat unanswered because she couldn't decide fast enough. Opportunities passed. And then fear crept in — would people eventually stop asking? Would her hesitation cost her a relationship?

Leisa's experience reminds me of the movie *Runaway Bride*.[1] On the surface, it's about a woman who can't commit — even down to something as small as how she likes her eggs. But underneath, it's not really about indecision at all. It's about a woman who had learned that decisions were something to be feared. She had been taught not to trust herself but instead to base her actions on the fear others had projected around her. These "protections" quietly rewrote her instincts until she no longer trusted her own voice or her abilities.

Leisa's paralysis had nothing to do with what she was making the decisions about, but rather, it reflected the negative belief underneath: Making a mistake wasn't safe.

---

1   Garry Marshall, *Runaway Bride*, Paramount Pictures,1999.

Eventually, tired of living without peace, she reached a breaking point. She began asking herself different questions:

Why can't I trust myself?

Why does every decision feel so heavy?

Why do I keep waiting for certainty that never comes?

And slowly, something shifted in her beliefs.

Leisa began to understand that, despite the way she had been raised, *discernment doesn't require fear*, and faith doesn't demand perfect clarity before movement. Sometimes God's guidance feels like a quiet nudge, not a flashing sign.

Learning to trust her instincts didn't mean she'd never be wrong. She simply no longer believed that being wrong would ruin her. Decision by decision, she practiced choosing with peace instead of panic. She told herself that making mistakes was fine. It meant she was learning and doing new things. The paralysis gradually disappeared, replaced by confidence and curiosity.

I could relate to Leisa's story. During some seasons, when I knew exactly what God was nudging me toward, and though I had the skills, the desire, and the confirmation, fear still whispered, "Wait." For months, maybe even years, I stood at the crossroads of comfort and calling. Every time I thought I'd made a decision, fear handed me a new reason to second-guess myself.

I prayed for signs, but when the signs came, I questioned them. I told myself I needed more clarity, more time, more certainty... when really, I was avoiding the discomfort of moving without guarantees.

YOU CAN LEARN TO TRUST YOURSELF

If these examples ring true for you — replaying decisions at night, waiting too long to respond, praying for clarity but fearing action — you're not weak or unfaithful. You're conditioned. This

Facet is about learning the difference between wisdom and fear and permitting yourself to trust that God can meet you, even if the path unfolds one step at a time, leaving the rest unseen.

What Indecisiveness Looks Like

Working on this Facet may help you if you're feeling:

- Stuck between multiple "right" choices and afraid of choosing one you'll later regret.
- Exhausted from overthinking even the smallest decisions.
- Afraid of disappointing someone or facing consequences if you choose for yourself.
- Caught in mental loops after decisions are made, replaying and second-guessing.
- Unsure how to trust your intuition versus fear or anxiety.
- Ready to move forward but unable to take the next step with peace.

What Polishing This Facet Will Bring

This Facet will help you:

- Trust your discernment instead of your fear.
- Make aligned decisions without needing perfect certainty.
- Recognize overthinking as conditioning, not wisdom.
- Learn to recognize God's guidance through quiet nudges instead of loud signs.
- Separate intuition from anxiety and urgency.
- Choose peace over paralysis even when the outcome isn't guaranteed.
- Stop second-guessing every movement.

You can have peace, not panic, after a decision. You can be confident even without full clarity. You can move forward without emotional whiplash.

How We'll Get There

The next eight Sparks of Wisdom will help you learn how to:

- Change your mindset to quiet the internal noise of doubt, fear, and second-guessing.
- Understand how past conditioning shapes present hesitation.
- Release the negative belief that being wrong is unsafe or unforgivable.
- Build confidence in your ability to decide and recover.
- Take small, faithful steps without waiting for guarantees.
- Experience the truth that clarity often comes *after* obedience.

Decision paralysis isn't so much about the choice in front of you as it is about the fear-based story underneath that choice. This Facet is meant to help you break free of that story — not through recklessness, but through building the trust that even if you stumble, you will not fall out of God's care.

A diamond may form through pressure, but what allows it to shine is its cut — a decisive strike along the right plane. In the same way, your life isn't shaped by waiting; it's shaped by faithful movement. One aligned decision can bring more clarity than years of overthinking. That single cut could help shape your diamond for a brilliant display.

LET THE VISION HAVE THE FINAL SAY

Have you ever felt the tug to learn something new — take a class, finish a certification, or complete the degree you once hit pause on —but the application sits untouched, quietly accusing you from across the room? Maybe you started a family, chose a different path, or life simply pulled you in another direction. And now, even though the desire is still there, you tell yourself you're too old, too busy, or already too far behind. So, the application sits. And so does your dream.

You make a pros-and-cons list and (let's be honest) the pros always win on paper, but those cons whisper more loudly. They're easier to listen to because they offer a comfortable escape route, keeping you safe. They tempt you to settle instead of stretch.

Yet that ache — that holy whisper that says *you were made for more* — keeps resurfacing. After all, you asked for that application for a reason. And so, you're caught between hope and despair... and you can't move.

What's the worst thing that could happen? Maybe you won't get accepted. But what if you will? Let's build a vision of that.

Can you picture yourself one year from now — certification complete, confidence restored, and you, transformed into the next brilliance-filled version of yourself?

This is where diamonds are formed: in the decision to keep going, even when uncertainty begs you to stay still. So, ask yourself: Do you want what's in the vision? Is playing it safe worth giving that up one more day, or one more week? Are you still okay with allowing those days and weeks to grow into years?

Sometimes the hardest part of growth is simply starting — especially when an application, opportunity, or dream feels intimidating. The fear of not finishing or being "too late" keeps many women stuck. But the tug you feel is proof that God placed the desire in your heart for a reason, and your future self is waiting for you to take the first step.

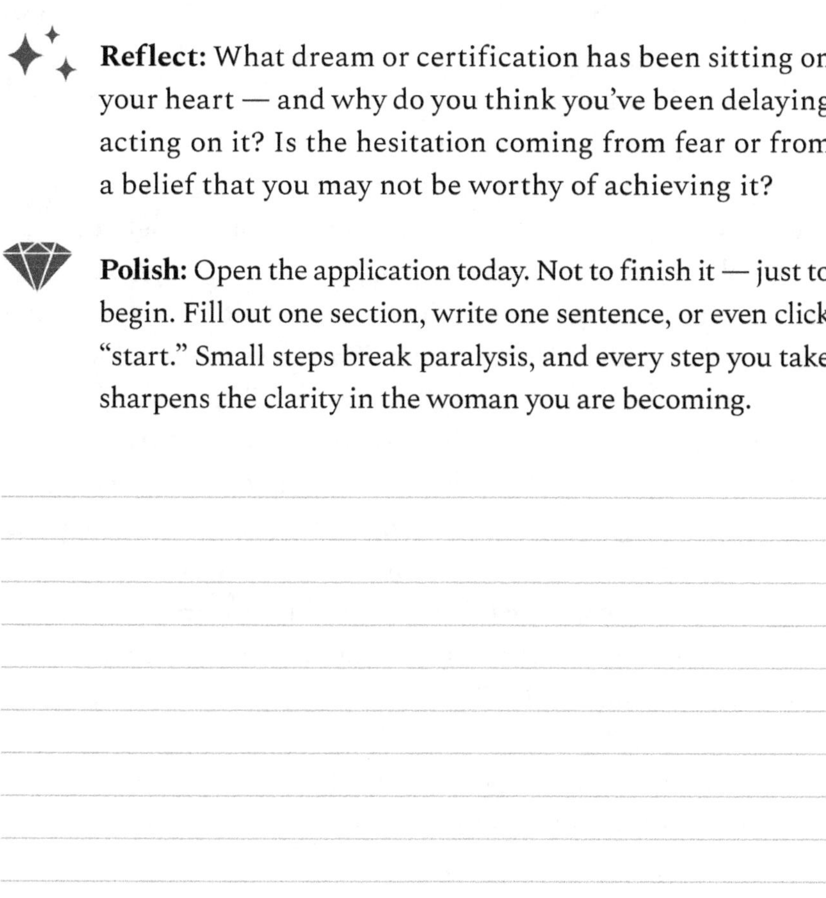

Reflect: What dream or certification has been sitting on your heart — and why do you think you've been delaying acting on it? Is the hesitation coming from fear or from a belief that you may not be worthy of achieving it?

Polish: Open the application today. Not to finish it — just to begin. Fill out one section, write one sentence, or even click "start." Small steps break paralysis, and every step you take sharpens the clarity in the woman you are becoming.

FOCUS ON THE FIT

When you're trying to decide what to do next, you can get lost in the noise of priorities — yours and those of others — all clamoring for attention. It can seem like you have no choice because everything is equally important. There's no clear right answer. They're all potentially right and also potentially wrong.

It reminds me of what decorating my house feels like. Why is the decorating process so hard for so many of us? Between layouts, color schemes, patterns, scale, and price tags, we can feel lost in a maze of decisions where every choice has this "right and wrong" quality. Home renovation shows make it look easy — hideous turns to stunning in minutes. Even seeing my old house online after it sold, with a totally different furniture layout, had me thinking, *"WOW... I wish I would've thought of that!"*

But truthfully? I hate change when it requires a dozen decisions.

I have even tried to hire decorating help because I couldn't see past what was already there. In the meantime, I hung some pictures and rearranged what I could. Then a friend with design vision walked in and said, "Wow, you should fire your decorator!"

And I just laughed... because the decorator was *me*.

It may not have looked perfect to her, but it worked in the moment. And I gained knowledge I could use later. I may not have been a master decorator, but I was definitely having a better time than when I was too terrified to do anything.

And that's when it clicked: Learning is part of the process. And it can be fun if you let it. Sometimes your decision won't be right for everyone else — but if it feels right to *you*, that's what creates transformation. And that transformation, not perfect skills from the start, is part of what creates the whole — in my case, a home. The same applies to your business or your other goals.

Just focusing on the fact that you did something that worked in the moment can create confidence, no matter what anyone else thinks.

Clarity doesn't come from choosing what everyone else loves. It comes from trusting your own eye, your own taste, your own brilliance, and what fits *you* — and having fun learning in the process.

Your decisions don't have to be perfect to be powerful —
they only have to be right for you. Trust your own vision,
even when you can't see the whole "layout" yet.
Confidence grows each time you choose.

Reflect: Where in your life are you waiting for someone else to approve the "layout" (or whatever the decision is about) instead of trusting your own eye, instincts, and brilliance?

Polish: Choose one small area — a room, a corner, a habit, or a decision — and make a choice today *without outsourcing your confidence to someone else's validation.* Trust yourself enough to pick, place, or begin. And then do it!

THE RIGHT TIME IS NOW

For years, I carried a quiet desire to renew my wedding vows. So much had been rebuilt, deepened, and refined that it just felt right.

I loved my husband differently than I did at twenty. My love felt stronger. Freer. More intentional.

I imagined our children standing beside us, witnessing not just a marriage, but a love that had grown through seasons, pressure, forgiveness, and faith.

I even bought the dress. I gifted myself a new ring after twenty years — a symbol of the woman I am now. And I knew I wanted the event blessed in church.

And yet... we never set the date.

I told myself I was "waiting for the right timing." That sounded so practical. But the truth underneath was that I was afraid to make the decision *and do it.*

What if people don't understand? What if they think it's too indulgent? What if I can't explain why it matters so much?

Listening to these negative inner voices, I held the dream at bay instead of honoring it. But the thought was always there, and I started talking about it with friends and family. In my head, if I talked about it enough, making the decision to plan it would become easier and less judged.

Decision paralysis often hides behind fear, wearing a reasonable mask. The fear isn't even necessarily that we will fail — sometimes it's the fear of allowing ourselves to want something deeply and letting it be seen. It's a fear of expressing authenticity.

The moment I realized this wasn't about timing, but about permission, I looked at my husband and said, "Let's pick a date." I wasn't waiting for the right time anymore. I was choosing it. Hopefully, my dress will still fit in September of 2028, our 25th anniversary!

Sometimes the hardest decisions to make are the ones closest to your heart. And yet, when you allow fear to guide you instead of honoring your true self, you lose so much opportunity. When you allow yourself to celebrate the brilliance God has been shaping in you all along, your entire life gains a deeper meaning that fear can never bring.

Reflect: What desire have you been delaying because you're afraid it won't be celebrated, understood, or perfect enough?

Polish: Do one thing today that turns this dream from "someday" into motion — a text, a date, a draft. Confidence follows action, not the other way around.

QUIET THE NOISE TO HEAR THE NUDGE

With all the information we have at our fingertips — Google reviews, books on every topic, social media full of opinions — you'd think decisions would be easier. But somehow, all that noise often makes it worse. It leaves us drowning in variables and too many possibilities. Along with promising examples of how something has worked for someone else, we see just as many that ended in failure.

Even when the outlook is promising, we doubt it. We tell ourselves, *"But what if my situation is different? What if it goes wrong for me?"*

Armed with all that "helpful" information, we lie awake replaying every possible outcome of a decision. We list the pros and cons, convince ourselves we're ready, and then suddenly fear slips in and steals every ounce of momentum. One moment we're confident, and the next we're spiraling through ten different "what if" scenarios that leave us overwhelmed and frozen.

However, if we listen more deeply, there's often a different feeling underneath all the noise. For me, it's a flutter in my stomach or a wave of dizziness that isn't nerves — it's the Holy Spirit. The nudge I've learned to recognize. The gentle whisper that says, *"I'm here. Trust Me."*

If you learn to tune into this, everything changes. Peace comes when we choose to trust that God will guide, redirect, and protect us — even if we can't see the full picture yet.

You don't have to have every answer. You just need the courage to listen.

Decision paralysis grows in the space where fear and overthinking meet. But when we quiet the noise and trust the Holy Spirit's nudge, clarity becomes less about certainty and more about faith.

Reflect: What decision are you currently overthinking, and what fear is truly hiding beneath all your "what if" scenarios? Now, listen more deeply. Under the fear, do you also feel a quiet nudge? If so, what does it feel like? How is it different from the fear? What is it telling you?

Polish: Pause today and pray for one simple thing: *direction for the next right step.* Not the whole plan — just the next step. Then take one small action in that direction, trusting God to guide you the rest of the way.

YOUR CALLING IS YOUR AUTHORITY

Sometimes the wildest ideas come to us in the quiet moments — drifting off, waking up, or somewhere between sleep and prayer. And we wonder: *Was that just a dream, or was it a nudge?*

Some dreams fade when the sun rises. Others won't leave you alone.

I'll never forget the nap where I dreamt of opening my boutique. I woke up, felt the spark, and took action almost immediately. And I've always wondered — how many beautiful things in life begin as a whisper like that? We hear it, and we act. We can't help it because it seems so important.

However, what happens when we don't act right away? Most of us have dreams we've tucked away. Dreams that felt too big, too risky, too financially scary, or too selfish. Dreams we tell ourselves we'll revisit later — *when the kids are older, when money is better, when the house is paid off, when life slows down.*

And then months turn into years.

And years turn into "maybe it wasn't meant for me."

A deferred dream doesn't disappear — it dims. And every time you put it off, it moves one step further from your heart.

Yet when God plants an idea in you — that spark, that excitement, that undeniable tug — it's not random. It's refinement. It's preparation. It's Him sharpening the edges of a new Facet on your diamond, inviting you into transformation.

Fear will always give you an excuse to wait. Faith invites you to move.

Even if your dream seems impossible right now, take authority for making it happen. Don't let the dream God placed in your heart become the dream you leave behind. He gave it to you for a reason. Look for a way. Ask for more help. Even those small things are ways of taking action. And if He brought you to it, He'll get you through it.

A deferred dream doesn't disappear — it dims. If God placed the idea on your heart and it keeps returning, trust that it's more than imagination; it may be an invitation. Don't wait so long that fear eventually wins over faith.

Reflect: What dream keeps resurfacing in your heart, no matter how much you try to dismiss or delay it?

Polish: Write down one small, brave step you can take toward this dream — research, a conversation, a prayer, or a commitment — and do it today. Momentum creates clarity.

DECISIVENESS SPARK 6:

LISTEN FOR THE NUDGE

Sometimes we think we know what's right for us, but we're missing something important. In those cases, God's nudge needs to temporarily override our own decision.

We can recognize the opportunities when they're big — an investment, a business partnership, a chance to change the direction of your life. Yet many opportunities aren't the big, dramatic moments. Sometimes they're small, gentle invitations — a friend asking you to lunch, an event that feels too far away or too expensive, a phone call you keep meaning to make, an inner nudge toward a dream you almost pursue but talk yourself out of.

No matter how big or small, every opportunity carries a ripple. A choice. A reaction in the web God uses to tie everything together.

Recently, I invited a friend to an event she really didn't want to attend. Her excuses were valid — time, cost, overwhelm — but something in her spirit tugged. She came anyway. And it turned out she was *exactly* where she was meant to be. She had been feeling the nudge from God for a while that she should take a leap of faith in her business but wasn't sure if it was the right decision. At the event, she heard exactly what she needed to feel confident that she was on the right path and was excited to move forward.

The stories in that room were woven together in ways none of us could have planned — connections, timing, breakthroughs — webs only God could weave. Even the conversation threads after the event were unmistakably divine. Not coincidence... coordination.

If you trace back the biggest blessings in your life, you'll probably see the same thing — a series of tiny yeses, unexpected turns, and "accidental" moments that only make sense looking backward.

So, if you feel the tug to call someone, to say yes to an invitation, to take a chance on yourself, don't let fear or hesitation steal what God may be orchestrating. Sometimes the smallest step toward yes becomes the moment that shapes your entire path.

Missed opportunities aren't always big — sometimes they're the small yeses we talk ourselves out of. When we follow the tug God places on our hearts, we step into the divine web He's weaving. Your next yes just might connect you to your next breakthrough.

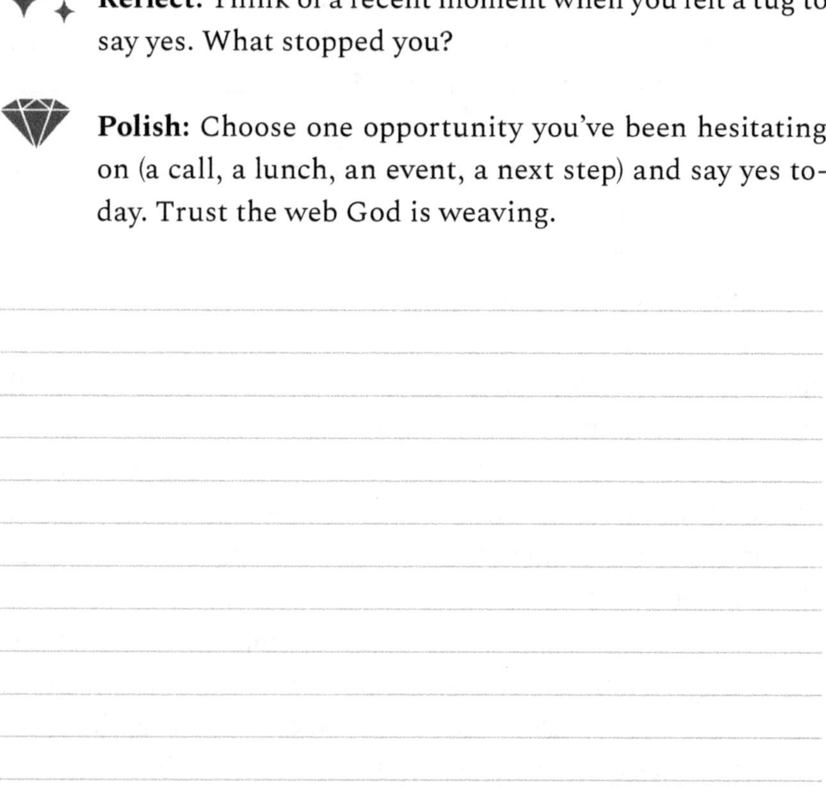

Reflect: Think of a recent moment when you felt a tug to say yes. What stopped you?

Polish: Choose one opportunity you've been hesitating on (a call, a lunch, an event, a next step) and say yes today. Trust the web God is weaving.

LEARN TO READ THE SIGNS

Have you ever begged God for a sign — any sign — that you were making the right choice? I used to pray for a bright neon arrow pointing in the exact direction I should go. Something loud. Obvious. Impossible to miss.

But the funny thing is that the signs were there all along. I just wasn't paying attention. Or in reality, I was hoping for a more dramatic delivery.

I used to wish I could hear the audible voice of God telling me exactly what to do, step by step. But looking back, I realize I *was* hearing Him — not through words, but through nudges, peace, discomfort, "coincidences," and moments that aligned far too perfectly to be accidental.

When I read back through my old journals, I'm always amazed by how many prayers He answered, how many situations worked out in ways I never expected. In the moment, it felt like nothing was moving. But now I can see how His timing was perfect, and His guidance was steady.

Yes, it's hard to tell the difference between God's plan and our free will. Because God already knows the choices we'll make — and He loves us through them. He redirects us when needed, shifts things for our good, and continues piecing the puzzle together even when we wander off the path.

We don't walk alone. He guides, even in silence.

The signs are often there even when we can't see them.
God guides us gently — through nudges, peace, and timing —
not because our choices are perfect, but because His love is.

Reflect: When you look back at past prayers or decisions, where can you now see God's fingerprints — moments you misunderstood then but recognize clearly now?

Polish: Re-read an old journal entry, prayer note, or memory from a hard season. Write down one way God showed up in that situation, even if it wasn't obvious at the time.

LEAP WITH FAITH

Sometimes clarity doesn't come before the decision; it comes because of it. One bold step can unlock a kind of peace and momentum you didn't even realize you were craving.

For an entire year, I knew deep down that my boutique was no longer bringing me joy. I loved my customers and adored my employees, but joy had turned into duty and duty into heaviness. Still, I couldn't let go. I thought maybe I should sell it, so I prayed: "God, if selling isn't what You want, show me."

And He did. Fast.

Almost overnight, the energy shifted. The busiest seasons suddenly became the slowest. Foot traffic dried up. It felt like an invisible barrier had been placed over the door. At the same time, my other businesses blossomed, pulling my attention to where God needed me next.

I remember sharing all of it with my coach. She listened quietly and then asked one simple question: "What's stopping you?"

That question cracked something open inside me. It was exactly what I needed to hear — the confirmation that the step I had been afraid to take was the step God had been preparing me for all along.

Closing the boutique wasn't just a business decision. It was an act of obedience. A bold first step and a leap of faith into the woman I was becoming.

Bold steps often bring the clarity that fear tries to hide.
When we move with faith, God meets us with direction,
momentum, and peace we didn't know we needed.

Reflect: Where in your life have you been delaying a decision even though your peace has already left the situation?

Polish: Write down one decision you've been avoiding. Then list the signs, nudges, or shifts that may already be pointing you toward your next bold step. And ask God for a sign if you haven't seen any.

FOCUS

Let all things be done decently and in order. — 1 Corinthians 14:40

"I'm doing all the things. Why am I getting nowhere?"

Scattered energy sneaks in quietly. You say yes because you can, because you're capable, because people depend on you. You juggle, you perform, you show up, you pour out. Before you know it, you're overwhelmed, and no matter how much you do, you never feel caught up, fulfilled, or focused.

It may look like productivity from the outside, but inside, it feels like you're running in circles. And sometimes you don't notice the toll it's taking on you until it starts to affect your life in negative ways, such as health crises or relationship problems.

Mollie learned this the hard way.

She is the nurse everyone depends on. She works long shifts, picks up extra hours, and goes in on her days off because she can't stand the thought of anyone feeling alone or uncared for. She's also a mom — one who quietly grieves how much of her children's lives she's missed because work always came first. It wasn't what she would have chosen, but as a single mom, she did what she had to do.

For years, driven by her desire to fill everyone else's needs, Mollie lived in motion. Eating on the run. Living on caffeine. Carrying stress that never really left. Her health declined, her relationships became strained, and her nervous system was constantly on edge.

At night, when the house was finally quiet, she escaped into books, which felt steady and always took her someplace else. She sometimes reached for alcohol to take the edge off the emotional weight she'd been carrying alone.

Then one day, the anxiety hit so hard she thought she was having a heart attack. She ended up in the emergency room, scared, exhausted, and overwhelmed. And even in that moment, she struggled to believe she deserved care. Instead, the familiar questions surfaced.

Why can't I catch a break?

Why is this happening to me now?

What will happen to my patients if I can't be there?

Mollie had grown up in a home with parents whose attention always seemed focused elsewhere. Forgotten, unseen, and uncared for, she learned to become for others what she herself needed. She never wanted them to feel the way she did.

But beneath the caregiving, the strength, and the responsibility, Mollie is still that little girl — longing to be chosen and to be seen, to find safety and rest, and to be valued and cared for as she tries so hard to do for others.

When do I get a choice?

Am I not important, too?

Doesn't anyone care about me?

This is the quiet wound that can scatter your focus: the idea that others are more important than yourself. That they always come first — even at your own expense.

If parts of Mollie's story feel familiar, it's time to look differently at yourself. If you feel like you're not achieving your purpose because you have too many conflicting priorities, or you've learned to be strong, dependable, and selfless at the cost of your own needs, if rest feels uncomfortable and being cared for feels unfamiliar, this Facet is for you.

However, you don't need help learning how to do more and complain less. What you need is a reminder to remember your self-worth and put the oxygen mask on yourself first, like they tell you in an airplane.

You might be terrified of failing others — but the true problem is that you've been carrying more than you were ever meant to carry alone, for far too long. And it's time to change that.

It's simple. Like with that oxygen mask on the airplane, you need to ensure your own needs are met first. Self-care is vital. If you don't care for yourself, you won't be able to show up for others.

When you view your own needs as being equal to those of others, you'll not only be more fully present for them, but you'll also be able to relax and enjoy your life more. And you deserve that, too.

This Facet is your affirmation: You are worthy of rest and self-care, and your needs are important.

IT'S TIME TO REFOCUS

This Facet can sometimes seem like lack of purpose, but the root cause is different. With unclear purpose, you're questioning why you're here and trying to understand why you're not feeling fulfilled. With focus issues, on the other hand, you may be grounded in your purpose but still unfulfilled because you aren't effectively achieving it.

What Scattered Focus Looks Like

Your struggles may relate to scattered focus if you feel any of the following:

- Pulled in ten directions at once.
- Overcommitted, overextended, overwhelmed, frustrated, and discouraged.
- Constantly busy but not moving forward.
- Emotionally drained despite "doing everything right."
- Easily distracted or derailed.
- Afraid of slowing down because stillness feels uncomfortable.
- Afraid of saying no and disappointing others.

Your world may look full — but *you* don't feel full.

What Polishing Your Focus Can Bring

Working on this Facet will help you:

- Feel clear and centered.
- Create boundaries without guilt.
- Know where your energy is best invested.
- Do less, but achieve more.
- Feel grounded instead of scattered.
- Use your gifts with intention and purpose.

When you're aligned and comfortable with where you're directing your energy, you can finally achieve productivity, yet retain your peace. You'll feel a freedom from all of the "shoulds," allowing you to focus on action that actually builds momentum. You can say yes to what matters and let the rest go.

How We'll Get There

The eight Sparks of Wisdom in this Facet will help you learn how to:

- Identify where your energy is leaking.
- Release the pressure to do it all.
- Reclaim your time, clarity, and focus.
- Use your ambition in ways that fuel you rather than drain you.
- Step into a life that feels intentional instead of reactive.

This is where you stop trying to do everything and start becoming *effective* — aligned, purposeful, and powerful.

A diamond's brilliance doesn't come from light alone; it also springs from the precision of its cut, directing light into order. Scattered light diffuses and dims, while focused light dazzles.

Your energy works the same way. If your efforts are not aligned with your true calling, your energy becomes scattered and ineffective, its results diffuse and dim. You were never created to be everything for everyone, scattering your light in too many places and dimming its brilliance. By aligning with your purpose, you direct your energy with precision, transforming chaos into clarity, scatter into sparkle. Focusing your energy where it matters, including leaving space for yourself, isn't selfish. It's stewardship.

CLARIFY THE LOAD

It's 3 a.m. You wake up, stare at the ceiling, and try to will your mind to settle... but it doesn't.

So, you do what you know you shouldn't — you reach for your phone. The screen burns your eyes, but your brain is already buzzing.

You start the list....

The tasks you forgot.

The ones waiting for you tomorrow.

The groceries.

The email you meant to send.

The uniform that needs to be washed.

The bill you meant to pay.

The drawer you swore you'd organize last summer.

And like clockwork, as soon as you see everything you still haven't finished, the mental loop begins.

You're way behind. You should be doing more every day.

Why didn't you remember that?

How will you get all of this done?

Maybe you've even convinced yourself these nights are productive. That you do your best thinking at 3 a.m. (And on the days when you're not up that early, you find yourself yelling at Siri while in the shower, telling her to set a reminder for something else you forgot.)

You cross off ten things... add twelve more... and still feel behind.

It's not just the list that drains you. It's the belief that your worth is tied to completing it.

When you pause — really pause — you might notice something tender buried beneath the chaos: Most of the things on your list aren't about tasks. They're about love. They're about caring for the people and spaces that shape your world. They're about the unseen ways you show up, day after day.

But you don't have to carry them all at once.

Some things can wait. Some can even fall off the list entirely. And others were never yours to carry in the first place.

Your worth isn't measured by your to-do list. Sometimes, the most productive, life-giving thing you can do is give yourself permission to simply go back to sleep.

*Serving is sacred — but sacrificing yourself to keep
everyone else comfortable is not God's plan for you.
Every no you say to what drains you creates room for
a bigger yes that's more aligned with your purpose.*

Reflect: Where are you serving from obligation instead of from your calling — and what is it costing you?

Polish: Look at your current commitments and choose one volunteer role, committee, or recurring task to release. Free that time and energy so you can say yes to what God is actually preparing you for.

MANAGE THE CHECKLIST MANIA

How many tabs do you have open right now?

I just looked at my phone — Safari says 148. My computer? At least 12. And if I ever have to reboot? Oh no, it's all over!

Do you ever feel like your brain is running the same way? Half-finished ideas, no clear focus, jumping from one thought to the next — *squirrel!*

Most people love a good checklist. There's something satisfying about seeing everything laid out — the errands, the emails, the reminders. If we can start our day with a list, it feels like we are in control. We can check a box, close a tab, move to the next one.

But what if the reason we are still exhausted isn't that we are doing too much but that we never *close* anything fully?

Think about it. Even when we are resting, the tabs are still open — the conversation replaying in our head, the dream we haven't made time for still calling, the worry we can't quite name lingering in the background.

Maybe instead of another checklist, what our minds really need is a clean slate. A digital *and* emotional reboot. A moment to breathe, to say, "This can wait," and close one small tab — just for peace of mind.

When we do, we will find that focus again. And peace. And even a little joy, hiding under the noise.

Sometimes the most important tab to close is the one in your mind.
Give yourself permission to pause and reset.

Reflect: What tabs are still open in your mind right now? Which ones could you close — or at least minimize — to create more space for calm, creativity, and clarity?

Polish: What can you do today based on this reflection? What tab — worry, task, or unfinished thought — can you consciously close today to give yourself mental space to breathe?

LET OTHERS SERVE TOO

It was 2012, and I was leading the MOPS (Mothers of Preschoolers) group at church. I was a young mom with three little ones, working full-time, leading the group, and volunteering for every organization that asked.

I was stretched thin — exhausted, resentful, but still smiling. Because I *loved* to help. I wanted to be dependable and the one everyone could count on.

But one day, while I was venting to a friend about how overwhelmed I felt, she said something that changed everything:

"You need to say *no* so someone else can say *yes*."

At first, I laughed because that sounded impossible. I thought saying *no* meant letting people down, being selfish, or disappointing someone who was counting on me.

But she went on, "You're blocking someone else's opportunity. There's someone out there just as capable, maybe even more passionate, but they haven't had the chance to be asked yet."

That stuck with me.

So, I tried it. I said no and without apology. And do you know what happened? Someone else said yes. And they did a beautiful job. Maybe even better than I would have, because they *wanted* to be there. What drained me filled them.

That's when I realized — it works both ways. Every time I say yes to something that drains me, I'm saying no to the things that fill me. Saying yes to the wrong things is a lose-lose for everyone.

Now, I try to pause before agreeing to anything and ask myself one question: "Does this bring me closer to who I'm becoming, or does it pull me away?"

If it aligns with my values and purpose, that's an easy *yes*. If it doesn't — that's a graceful *no*.

When you say yes to everything out of guilt or obligation, you quietly say no to what actually fuels you. Learning to say no creates space for others to step in — and brings your focus back to the life, purpose, and peace you're meant to steward.

Reflect: When have you said yes out of guilt, obligation, or fear — and ended up resenting it later? How would it have felt to give someone else the gift of saying yes instead?

Polish: What can you do today based on this reflection? What priority could you honor by saying no to something that no longer fits and saying yes to what brings you joy, peace, or purpose?

LEAVE SPACE FOR YOU

Have you ever noticed that when you try to do everything, you end up doing nothing well? We tell ourselves we're great multitaskers, juggling schedules, responsibilities, and emotions. Unfortunately, no one really multi-tasks. We just switch focus faster, leaving a trail of half-finished tasks and forgotten appointments behind us.

Maybe you've double-booked yourself again. Maybe you're apologizing for being late... again. Maybe you're frustrated because you *know* you're capable, but you're simply stretched too thin.

Before you beat yourself up, pause. Ask yourself:

- *Why am I overfilling my schedule?*
- *Am I afraid to disappoint someone?*
- *Do I need a better system... or more courage to say no?*

You deserve margin in your day. Space to breathe. Space to catch up and to simply *be*. Try it! Leave some white space in your calendar. Schedule catch-up breaks and stretch moments between commitments. It's not lazy — it's leadership of self.

When your schedule is full, your life can feel empty.
Create space to breathe and remember yourself.

Reflect: What are you overcommitting to that causes unnecessary stress or chaos? What would change if you gave yourself permission to slow down and protect your time?

Polish: What can you do today based on this reflection? Which small shift — saying no, delegating, or creating space between tasks — can you practice today to bring more peace and focus into your day?

RECLAIM THE MOMENT

I keep telling myself, *"If I don't do it right now, I'll forget."* (And honestly, sometimes that's true!) But picking up my phone to send a quick text or email while we're sitting down to eat is my husband's biggest pet peeve.

(I always tried to defend myself by pointing out that the TV was on — but apparently, that's different.)

Truthfully, my husband has a point. When trying to multitask, I was only half there. Half of my attention was on what was happening at the table, while the other half was somewhere else — thinking about that email, that message, that "one more thing."

I was present, but not *really* there. And that meant I was missing out. I would often look up and realize all eyes were on me, waiting for a response. Or laughter would break out, and I completely missed the punch line. As much as I thought I could do both, I really could only be truly present in one conversation: My phone or my family.

Time with our kids, or even those quiet moments with our spouses, are too precious to be only half-present.

If you find this is an issue in your home, try leaving the phones in another room — just 30 minutes of real connection. It's a small change, but as the saying goes, it's never too late to start a new tradition. (Speaking of which, I'm going to push for turning the TV off too.)

Being fully present with those you love is worth more than checking one more thing off your list.

You may be physically present but mentally elsewhere, letting urgency steal the moments that matter most. Reclaiming your attention — especially in small, everyday spaces like the dinner table — restores connection, peace, and focus where it's needed most.

Reflect: Where in your life are you physically present but mentally elsewhere? It could be during family time, meetings, or even self-care moments. Awareness is the first step toward change.

Polish: Tonight, commit to one meal — no phones or other distractions. Just conversation, laughter, and connection. Notice how it feels to be *fully there*.

SAVOR DELAYS AS DEVELOPMENT TIME

If you're anything like most women, you have a sense of excitement for a new, beautiful planner or a fresh journal — the kind that feels full of possibility the moment you open it.

Or maybe you jot your thoughts in multiple notebooks, scribble prayers in the margins, or store ideas on your phone, only to forget where they all live.

All of these tasks and ideas and thoughts seem so full of potential, and they all want your attention. Unfortunately, you're only one person, and your time is limited. So, you hold onto them, even though you don't know when you'll achieve them.

And then, one day, you stumble upon an old page — a dream you wrote down, a prayer you whispered, a moment that once felt overwhelming — and you're reminded of something powerful: Seasons shift, even when you're convinced they never will.

Surprised, you realize that what you didn't have time for then, you can make room for now. And in fact, you know so much more today about how to make it happen that you can't wait to start.

When you look back, you might notice that often, what felt delayed wasn't denied — it was developing. God was weaving lessons and blessings together in ways that didn't make sense in the moment. What you once begged for didn't happen when you thought it should, but it came when you were ready to receive it.

Sometimes, the waiting season isn't wasted time. It's preparation, refinement, and alignment. It's the space between who you were and who you're becoming.

If you feel you're doing everything right and you still can't move your dream forward, take a moment to just breathe.

Instead of resenting the delay, honor it. Trust that God is moving pieces you can't see. Someday, you'll flip back through the pages and recognize the miracle that started with a pause.

"Someday" doesn't necessarily come when we wish for it, but it comes when we're ready.

Reflect: What dreams or prayers have you tucked into your own "someday" file? Are you waiting for the perfect time, or is God waiting for *you* to take the next step?

Polish: Find one old journal entry, note, or dream list and revisit it. Ask yourself: What has changed since then? What growth has happened? Then, choose one someday dream that still tugs at your heart and take one small, real step toward it *today.*

CLEAR YOUR MENTAL CLOSET

Remember that "roles closet" full of old identities that no longer fit? When our energy is scattered, it's often because we haven't done a mental closet-clearing recently. We don't realize we've picked up some new roles without looking at how they affect the expectations we shaped ourselves to in the past.

As you go through the Diamond polishing process, you'll find you still have old ideas lurking in the back of your mental closet, taking up space and energy. You may even still "put them on" and embody them without realizing it. If they are left over from your old default mode that told you to carry more than your share, it's time to reexamine them.

If you feel overwhelmed, it's not necessarily because you lack discipline or focus. It may be because you are quietly managing everyone else's needs, opinions, and unspoken expectations without realizing it. Somewhere along the way, you became the default helper. The dependable one. The woman who fills the gaps so things don't fall apart. Those old roles are still defining your priorities without you thinking about it. Over time, that constant outward pull fractures your attention and drains your peace. It can even make you resentful of things and people you care about.

Clarity begins when you name what is *yours* to hold — and what is not. To do that, you need to sort through your mental closet and start "donating" the roles that no longer fit.

While you're doing that, remember everything else you've learned in the other Facets, and release the guilt attached to stepping out of roles that no longer align with who you are becoming.

When you can discard these old habits without apologizing or feeling guilty, something settles inside you. The resentment fades, and the space fills with peace. Remember, you already have the decision-making authority. You just need to start using it to choose activities with clear intention.

And as we already know, a scattered light illuminates nothing. But a focused light? It dazzles.

It's all too easy to continue wearing an old role that sounded right long ago but scatters your energy today. To keep old habits from stifling new growth, take time now and then to intentionally sort through your role wardrobe and discard what no longer fits. Periodic realignment turns chaos into clarity.

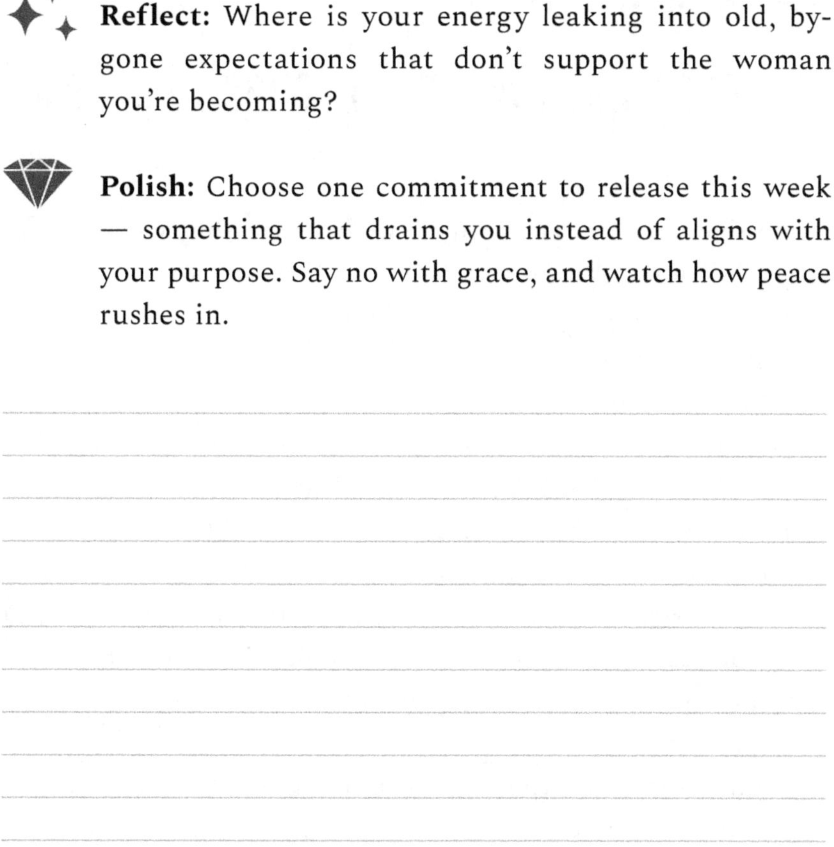

Reflect: Where is your energy leaking into old, bygone expectations that don't support the woman you're becoming?

Polish: Choose one commitment to release this week — something that drains you instead of aligns with your purpose. Say no with grace, and watch how peace rushes in.

RELEASE WHAT WAS NEVER YOURS TO CARRY

Some women struggle with focus because they've taken responsibility for things that were never meant to be theirs — things such as other people's emotions, outcomes, comfort, happiness, and success.

Does this ring a bell for you?

It often starts early in life. You learn to read the room. You sense what's needed before it's asked for. You step in, smooth things over, solve the problem, carry the weight.

At first, it looks like leadership, a demonstration of your maturity and strength. While those things may be your intent at first, they can go too far. Over time, something subtle happens. Your energy stops flowing toward your own life and begins orbiting everyone else's.

You manage the calendar. The feelings. The logistics. The expectations. You remember everything. You hold it all together.

And somehow, the things that matter most to *you* get pushed to the edges because you care so deeply about everyone else. Quietly, your focus begins to fracture.

When you believe it's your job to anticipate, prevent, fix, or carry what belongs to others, your attention is constantly pulled outward. You passively respond to everyone's needs without actively deciding anything. And the woman you are meant to become is left waiting for whatever scraps of energy remain.

As a high-capacity woman, you, like many others, were perhaps never taught this important lesson: **You are responsible TO people. You are not responsible FOR them.** As a wife and a mother, I often forget that if I don't let my husband and children do their own things, they will never learn.

At sixteen, I was able to buy a car, get insurance, register it, pay the tax, and balance a checkbook. By eighteen, I was able to find a rental home and get the utilities set up, all without the help of my parents. How? Because I had to. My parents weren't going to do it for me.

Somehow, though, as my kids reached that age, I felt bad making them do those things. Yet when they did, we always laughed that it was "doing BIG girl/boy things." And honestly, it felt great to release what was never mine to carry.

So, give yourself permission to stop asking, "Who needs me right now?" and start asking, "What am I being called to tend to in *my* life?"

You lose focus not because you lack discipline,
but because you've been carrying responsibilities that
are no longer yours to hold. When you release what belongs
to others and tend to what you're actually called to steward,
your energy returns, and your clarity sharpens.

Reflect: Where in your life are you carrying responsibility that belongs to someone else — emotionally, practically, or spiritually?

Polish: Choose one situation this week where you will pause before stepping in. Ask yourself: *Is this mine to carry, or am I allowed to let someone else rise?*

RELATIONSHIP

"As iron sharpens iron, so one person sharpens another." — *Proverbs 27:17*

"I've built a good life, but no one really gets me."

Loneliness is one of the most misunderstood experiences a businesswoman or leader can face. You can have a beautiful family, meaningful work, a full calendar, and a confident exterior yet still feel profoundly alone in the moments when the weight of your world rests quietly on your shoulders.

Success, visibility, and responsibility bring blessings, but they can also bring a unique kind of isolation. As I built businesses, mentored women, and led teams, the people around me often couldn't fully grasp the decisions I carried, the dreams I held, or the pressure beneath the surface. Everyone saw the highlight reel. Very few saw the heaviness underneath.

And maybe that's where you are too.

You're the strong one. The dependable one. The one people come to for answers, support, encouragement, leadership.

But who pours into *you*? Who understands the weight you carry, the expectations you juggle, the dreams that feel too big to say out loud?

I've been reading the same devotional for over five years now, and it still amazes me how the words can land differently every time. The passage always seems to meet me exactly where I am.

On this particular day, the page spoke about the pain of being hurt or betrayed by someone close — the kind of wound that cuts deepest because love and trust are involved.

It reminded me that while this may be one of the most painful experiences we endure, we cannot stay there. If we don't allow God to heal us and help us move beyond it, the pain doesn't stay contained — it begins to consume us. As said in Ephesians 4:32 (NIV), "Be kind and compassionate to one another, forgiving each other, just as in Christ God forgave you."

Being unable to forgive is more of a disease to our heart than the act that hurt us in the first place. Without forgiveness, we're left alone with bitterness and resentment, and over time, our ability to experience God's goodness and His plan for our lives becomes diminished, if not completely blocked.

That devotion felt like the perfect mirror for this Facet.

So often, I hear the stories of women who feel taken advantage of, overlooked, or repeatedly hurt — not once, but over and over again. And in those moments, wisdom doesn't always mean enduring more. Sometimes it means giving yourself permission to pause, to create distance, or to stop engaging in a relationship that no longer supports who you're becoming. Forgiveness doesn't require continued access. And healing doesn't always come from staying — sometimes it begins when you allow the relationship to change.

This story reminds me of the movie *Eat, Pray, Love*[2], where Julia Roberts plays Elizabeth Gilbert. It's based on a true story illustrating a woman's courage in stepping away from a romantic attachment to rediscover oneself.

---

2 Ryan Murphy, *Eat Pray Love*, Columbia Pictures, 2010.

In the movie's most powerful scene, Elizabeth and her husband are talking about the future. Their plans sound responsible and beautiful, but Elizabeth feels her chest tighten. Something inside her feels wrong.

She stares at the ceiling and listens to the fan hum. The room feels smaller than it did the day before. She tries to explain the ache, but the words won't cooperate. "I don't want this," she finally says, but what she really means is: "I don't recognize myself in this version of our life."

He is confused. Hurt. Defensive. An argument builds, not with shouting but misunderstanding. Love is present, but so is misalignment.

And then Elizabeth does something that feels small but it's powerful. She leaves the room. Not the marriage yet. Just the room. She walks into the bathroom and slides down the closed door. The cold tile brings her back to herself, and she starts crying. It's the messy, shoulders-shaking, breath-catching kind of crying from someone who has held it in for too long.

She looks up and simply says, "I don't know what to do. I'm lost." This moment doesn't change much externally. She's still married and in the same house, but she has stopped pretending. And that cold tile is the first solid thing she feels all day. She is finally choosing clarity. She isn't choosing to run away.

So, though the story contains a journey, the message isn't about travel or escape — it's about permission. You can give yourself permission to acknowledge that a relationship can be meaningful and still no longer be sustaining. You can choose growth without demonizing the past. You're allowed to step away even though you love someone, simply because you are no longer aligned with them.

The story reminds us that distance can be an act of wisdom. It grants us a pause that allows healing, clarity, and reconnection with self and God. If we choose a relationship again, we do it from a place of strength rather than sacrifice.

CREATE ALIGNED CONNECTIONS

When you stay in relationships that no longer support your growth, you go beyond loyalty and enter into self-betrayal. Real love doesn't require you to abandon yourself to keep the peace. It's time to examine your relationships and ensure you're creating connections that nurture everyone involved.

What Misaligned Relationship Looks Like

The reason I've named this Facet "relationship" instead of "relationships" is that the word "relationship" refers to the skill of relating, while your relationships are what you manage with that skill. In this Facet, we are talking about polishing the skill, so "relationship" is the word we need. However, the quality of your relationships does give you a good idea how your relationship skills measure up.

With that in mind, you may need to work on this Facet if you're feeling any of the following:

- Emotionally drained by relationships that once felt safe or familiar.
- Hurt, overlooked, or taken advantage of by the same person more than once.
- Conflicted between forgiving someone and continuing to give them access to you.
- Lonely even when surrounded by people.
- Like you've outgrown certain relationships but feel guilty admitting it.
- Unsure how to create distance without feeling unloving or disloyal.

What Polishing This Facet Will Bring

Working on this Facet will help you:

- Recognize and maintain the relationships that sharpen, support, and sustain you.
- Understand the difference between forgiveness and access.
- Create healthy boundaries without bitterness, guilt, or blame.
- Find peace in releasing relationships that no longer support who you're becoming.
- Be comfortable as relationships evolve.
- Experience relationships as nourishment, not obligation.

You'll find relationships that create mutual emotional safety instead of a need for self-protection. Instead of feeling pressure to give more than you are able, you'll foster mutual respect. Your relationships will focus on depth instead of performance. By building connections that strengthen rather than drain you, your relationship tension will be replaced with peace.

How We'll Get There

The next eight Sparks of Wisdom will help you:

- Heal relational wounds without hardening your heart.
- Release resentment that quietly isolates you.
- Discern which relationships need boundaries, distance, or renewal.
- Let go of the pressure to maintain connections that cost you your peace.
- Build a community aligned with who you are now, not who you used to be.
- Learn to connect from strength instead of duty.

Creating healthy distance can look different based on the situation. You don't necessarily need to cut someone off or walk away in anger. Maybe you just need to create some boundaries so you can hear your own voice again, heal what's been neglected, or become who you were always meant to be.

And from that place of strength, clarity, and self-respect, you can choose connection again — no longer out of fear or obligation, but from wholeness.

Diamonds are rarely found in isolation. They're formed in clusters that shape under shared pressure, strengthened side by side. And even the brightest diamond needs a setting to hold it steady, giving it just the right place to shine.

Similarly, your unique brilliance needs others to truly sparkle. The right relationships enhance and expand each individual's potential to dazzling proportions. This Facet invites you to recognize your Diamond Circle — the women who call you higher, hold you steady, and reflect your light back to you. You were never meant to achieve your calling alone.

SET LOVING BOUNDARIES

Maybe you've lived this too — the holiday that looks beautiful on the outside but quietly breaks your heart on the inside.

You take on the hosting to keep the peace. It isn't easy, but it simplifies the chaos and spares everyone else from discomfort. You're not sure how, but somewhere along the way, you became the one who holds the family together.

Every year, you pour your heart into making it special. You plan, shop, cook, and clean, rarely asking anyone to bring anything because you don't want to inconvenience them. You do it with love and intention because you want everyone to feel cared for.

But then the moment comes. People sit down, rush through the meal... and they're done, on to the next thing, without even a simple "Thank you," or an offer to help. These small gestures would mean more than they realize.

You try to swallow the frustration. You force a smile, smooth the tension. Yet, beneath it all is a quiet ache:

Does anyone see how much love I've poured into this?

People-pleasing often comes from a beautiful place — love, care, generosity. Yet it becomes exhausting when you give more than your heart can hold, yet you receive nothing that replenishes you.

In serving others, you're still allowed to set boundaries. You're allowed to ask for help and let others contribute. You're allowed to enjoy the celebration instead of managing every moment of it by yourself.

And you deserve peace — especially around the table you spend so much of yourself preparing.

Your effort doesn't lose value just because someone else fails to acknowledge it. And you are allowed to give from love without sacrificing yourself in the process.

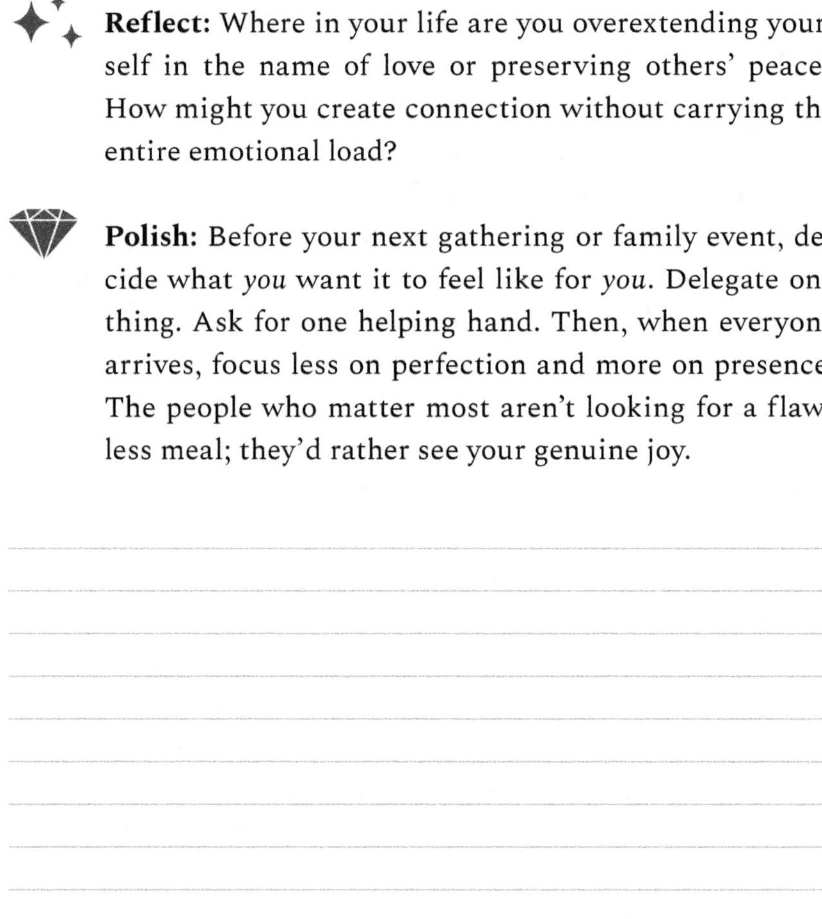

Reflect: Where in your life are you overextending yourself in the name of love or preserving others' peace? How might you create connection without carrying the entire emotional load?

Polish: Before your next gathering or family event, decide what *you* want it to feel like for *you*. Delegate one thing. Ask for one helping hand. Then, when everyone arrives, focus less on perfection and more on presence. The people who matter most aren't looking for a flawless meal; they'd rather see your genuine joy.

RELEASE WHAT HURTS YOU

How hard is it for you to let things go without apology?

Becky and I were friends for years — the kind of friendship people casually call "family." And for a long time, I held onto that title even when the relationship no longer felt safe, steady, or healthy. There were toxic traits, subtle digs, and emotional inconsistencies that left me feeling unsettled. But instead of protecting my own heart, I worried about hurting hers. I stayed friends with her longer than I should have because I didn't want to look mean.

The fact is that she had two versions of herself. One version was the fun, warm, carefree version I genuinely loved. The other was a guarded, unpredictable version shaped by a past she tried desperately to hide. I never knew which one I would get. And eventually, the strain of guessing started to take a toll.

When I chose to walk away, she had already begun drifting into a new friend group, yet I still felt guilty. I missed the real her when she showed up — the one who felt authentic, honest, and present. But I also knew I couldn't keep ignoring how the relationship made me feel.

Letting go wasn't easy. It rarely is. But releasing a toxic connection can bring clarity. You can pretend, or you can have real peace. I preferred emotional safety over walking on eggshells.

Sometimes the kindest thing you can do is stop forcing what no longer fits.

Letting go isn't mean — it's necessary. Releasing a toxic relationship creates space for connections that are healthy, steady, and aligned with who you're becoming.

Reflect: Where in your life are you holding onto a relationship out of guilt instead of genuine connection?

Polish: Give yourself permission to release one relationship, expectation, or obligation that drains you. Write a compassionate "closure statement" — even if you never send it — to free your heart from guilt and reclaim your peace.

FIND YOUR ALIGNED CIRCLE

Not many people truly understand the kind of drive, passion, or constant inner fire that pushes an entrepreneurial woman forward. When the people around you don't get it, you can feel misunderstood, out of place, or even alone. The higher I climbed in my personal growth and entrepreneurial journey, the more I began to feel the disconnect in certain friend circles.

Behaviors that once felt natural no longer aligned. When you're actively working to grow your faith, improve your character, and serve others with a pure heart, conversations start feeling different. You notice more: Gossip, small talk, jealousy, the subtle digs. They don't land the same. You no longer desire to shrink just to feel accepted. You want depth, honesty, encouragement — not comparison and competition.

Loneliness shows up in the small moments too — tucked inside the group chats.

If we opened our phones right now, most of us would laugh at the number of threads we're in. Group chats for work friends, mom friends, church friends, childhood friends, gym friends... our phones become a maze of conversations and circles.

Sometimes the loneliness isn't in the absence of group chats. It's in the awareness that there are some you're not included in.

The one where an invitation was sent that never reached you. The one where they started a new thread — without you. The one where someone needed to say something *about* you, so they made sure you wouldn't see it.

It's a sting that's hard to explain but impossible to ignore.

Sometimes the loneliness is simply the nudge from God that it's time to level up — to new rooms, new connections, and new friendships that match the woman you're becoming.

Not every circle can grow with you. When conversations shift and certain rooms no longer fit, it's not rejection — it's redirection. God removes you from the wrong group chats so He can place you in the right ones.

Reflect: Where in your relationships are you shrinking yourself to stay included — and what circle might God be inviting you to outgrow?

Polish: This week, mute one group chat that drains your energy and intentionally engage in a conversation (even a text) with someone who inspires you, supports you, or feels aligned with who you're becoming.

EMBRACE YOUR EVOLUTION TOGETHER

There comes a moment in a long marriage when you look across the table at your spouse and realize: You've changed. He's changed. Life has changed, and so has your identity inside it.

It's not a crisis or a failure. It's simply the quiet realization that years of parenting, working, serving, and running have reshaped who you are.

You've spent so long nurturing everyone else that you may have forgotten the parts of yourself your partner once fell in love with — the playful parts, the curious parts, the confident parts, the parts that existed before "Mom," "Wife," and "Organizer" took over.

If you've ever sat in the stillness of an evening and thought, "Where did *I* go?" you're not alone.

True reconnection requires you to do more than just improve your marriage — you must dig deeper and rediscover *yourself* inside the marriage.

If you're in a long-term relationship and you feel as if your identity has vanished, relax — it's still there. It's simply layered beneath responsibilities. Peeling those layers back can bring you home to yourself again.

After years of putting your children first, you may realize you've lost sight of who you are beyond motherhood and wifehood. Reconnecting with your husband can help you reclaim parts of yourself that were quietly set aside.

Reflect: Are you nurturing your own identity while nurturing your family? Could taking time to rediscover yourself through relationships be the action that lets your diamond reflect its full light? Where have you lost yourself in roles or relationships, and what part of your identity is waiting to be rediscovered?

Polish: Instead of assuming your partner "should know" who you are now, articulate it. Share one desire, dream, or change you've been quietly carrying.

FIND THE RIGHT GUIDES

You'd be surprised how many people besides athletes or CEOs have coaches. There are fitness coaches, speaking coaches, mindset coaches, dating coaches, health coaches, life coaches, and business coaches. And honestly, we all need someone who sees what we can't, someone who can guide us into the next best version of ourselves.

I've hired many coaches over the years — an inventory coach, a mindset coach, and most recently, a book coach to help me bring this message to life. Each one came into my life at exactly the right moment, with exactly the right expertise, when I needed someone more knowledgeable, more experienced, or simply more believing than I was in that moment.

I've learned that the greatest gift coaches give is clarity. It's awareness spoken out loud.

For me, three phrases from three different coaches changed everything:

"What's stopping you from closing the boutique?"

"Where does this belief that you're not enough come from?"

"You are the perfect person to write these stories — millions of women need you."

Those words cracked something open in me. They helped me see the path God had been gently nudging me toward all along. Sometimes we need someone from outside our world to say what we've been too afraid to admit — that the next chapter is waiting, and we're more ready than we think.

The right coach doesn't just guide you — they hold up a mirror to the woman God created you to be. Sometimes, one brave sentence spoken at the right moment becomes the doorway to your entire next chapter.

Reflect: What truth has someone spoken to you — recently or long ago — that you haven't fully allowed yourself to believe yet?

Polish: Identify one area of your life where you feel stuck or uncertain. Ask for guidance — whether from a coach, mentor, friend, or through prayer — and write down the one sentence you most need to hear right now.

SEEK SOUL-ALIGNED FRIENDSHIP

Have you ever wondered why it feels so hard to find *your person* —the one friend you can trust with your whole heart? For many women, that longing runs deep.

Maybe someone once told you to tone it down, be quieter, or stop being "too much." Maybe you've shared something vulnerable and been met with silence. Maybe parts of you learned to retreat, protect, or stay surface-level because honesty wasn't always safe.

Yet despite all of that, you may still carry that same desire from childhood, for a confidante who feels like home. You can picture her now. She listens without judgment. She celebrates the highs, sits with you in the lows, and says yes to your dreams even before you fully believe in them yourself.

We see these friendships on screen, in our favorite movies.

Firefly Lane[3], where childhood friends reconnect…

Steel Magnolias[4], where women hold each other together through every season…

Beaches[5], depicting the iconic bond that spans decades…

As we watch them, something inside us whispers, *I want that, too.*

If you've ever craved that kind of connection, you're far from alone. So many women are quietly longing for the exact friendship you're praying for. So many women want a safe place to

---

3   Maggie Friedman, *Firefly Lane*, Netflix, 2021–2023.

4   Herbert Ross, *Steel Magnolias*, TriStar Pictures, 1989.

5   Garry Marshall, *Beaches*, Touchstone Pictures, 1988.

land. So many women would love to share the kind of honesty, warmth, and loyalty you're ready to give.

Someone in your current circle may be praying for the same connection — and both of you might be waiting for the other to go first.

*You're not the only one longing for a friend
who feels like home. Many women are quietly
craving the same deep connection. Sometimes, all
it takes is one brave moment to open the door to it.*

Reflect: Who in your life feels like someone you could trust a little more — and what holds you back from letting yourself be seen by them?

Polish: Reach out to one woman who feels safe, kind, or promising. Invite her for coffee, a walk, or a simple conversation — and share one small, honest piece of your heart. Connection grows through tiny acts of courage.

MAKE A DIAMOND FRIEND

There are high achievers, and there are those who are perfectly content with a 9 to 5 and shutting off for the day. There's nothing wrong with either one. But those of us who strive for *more* need encouragement and connection with others who understand the high-potential mindset that never stops.

We're the women who juggle a dozen things at once, the ones people look at and say, "I don't know how you do it all." The truth is, we thrive with a goal in mind. We love the checklist, the progress, and the satisfaction of seeing something through to the finish.

Over the years, I've met many women who *get it*. Usually, it happens while I'm traveling or working. Rarely have I found those connections close to home.

Then I met Shae. A true Diamond Friend.

A business owner, a mom, a woman of faith, and a friend who keeps family time sacred yet embraces joy and purpose in her work. She's someone I can call to brainstorm big ideas, pitch a community project, or simply talk with about kids and family.

Meeting Shae led me to a network of Mompreneurs who meet regularly to grow, both in business and in life. We celebrate milestones, support each other through challenges, and remind one another that purpose and friendship can shine just as brightly as success.

Sometimes the connection we're missing isn't just about friendship — it's about being *seen* by someone who speaks our same language of drive, purpose, and faith.

Your first Diamond Friend reminds you that you don't have to shine alone. One authentic connection can change everything.

Reflect: Do you have a Diamond Friend? If not, do you know anyone who would be a good fit? How could you meet more Diamond Friends?

Polish: Reach out to one woman who inspires you. Start the conversation. That single connection could open the door to a whole community waiting to grow with you.

SAY YES TO WHO YOU'RE BECOMING

When you're a woman who leads, builds, carries, and keeps moving, loneliness doesn't always look like being alone. Sometimes it looks like being surrounded by people yet feeling unseen.

You're the strong one. The dependable one. The one who has it "together." And because of that, invitations from others can start to feel complicated.

A dinner.

A girls' night.

A casual gathering.

Your mind floods with reasons to stay home:

I won't fit in anymore.

No one really understands my world.

It feels easier to avoid the small talk.

So, you decline. You want connection, but it hasn't always felt safe or simple.

What happens if one day, you pause... and decide to say yes?

Not out of obligation but out of a quiet hope that maybe, just maybe, someone out there gets you — and now is your chance to find them. You show up feeling a little guarded, a little unsure... and then something unexpected happens.

You find yourself laughing. You find yourself opening up. You find yourself connecting with one person who sees past your title, your strength, your highlight reel.

One small yes has become a complete shift, a bridge between isolation and belonging. It's a reminder that you don't have to do life or leadership alone.

Sometimes the most life-changing moments begin with a single yes.
Say yes before you're ready — joy is waiting on the other side.

Reflect: What invitations have you been saying no to out of fear, habit, or self-doubt? What might open up for you if you say yes just once?

Polish: This week, say yes to one thing that stretches you. A coffee date, a class, a community event, something that reminds you you're part of something bigger. Don't let fear make your world smaller.

WHEN ALL SEVEN FACETS
ARE HONORED TOGETHER IN
A FULL EXCHANGE OF LIGHT,
BRILLIANCE EMERGES.

PART 4

Pulling It All Together

This final section is where everything comes together. Here, you step back and see how each Facet you've worked through — Identity, Purpose, Self-Worth, Authenticity, Decisiveness, Focus, and Relationships — is meant to function as part of a living, breathing whole. When one Facet is ignored, the rest can't reach their true potential, and the diamond dulls. When they are honored together in a full exchange of light, brilliance emerges.

In this section, you will learn how to manage all the Facets in balance, noticing when one area is throwing the others off, and realigning without self-judgment. Brilliance is the skill of living with peace, joy, and clarity so fully that your presence gives others permission to do the same. This is leadership from wholeness. Its impact not only changes your own life; it quietly, powerfully, and unmistakably changes the world around you.

BRILLIANCE

For God, who said, "Let light shine out of darkness," made his light shine in our hearts to give us the light of the knowledge of God's glory displayed in the face of Christ." — 2 Corinthians 4:6

**"I've done the work — now,
how do I live my truth consistently?"**

Brilliance requires work to integrate and understand all parts of yourself. No matter how a single part shines, until all the Facets work together, the whole diamond can't achieve its full sparkle.

By now, you've learned how to recognize your patterns, honor your values, protect your energy, and show up with more conviction and less fear.

Now, we'll learn more about integration — how those lessons live in your everyday life and how they expand outward to others, too.

What do I mean by "brilliance"? It's the quiet confidence of knowing how to return to yourself. It's the way your peace ripples outward. It's the moment your growth stops being private and starts empowering others.

That's how Oriana's story unfolded. She's a beautiful example of what happens when a woman gives herself permission to let all her Facets align, finally allowing herself to shine.

Oriana was in the trenches of motherhood and postpartum depression when one day, a close friend walked in. Oriana couldn't help noticing something different about her.

A spark.

Her friend had just had her colors done. Something about the process had changed her in an indefinable way. She carried herself differently, seemed more comfortable with herself.

And in that moment, Oriana realized what she had been missing: her own spark, which had been dimmed and hidden for years.

She immediately set her own appointment with me. Later, she confessed, "I was so impressed by the boldness, the expression, the unapologetic way you showed up," she told me later. "I have always admired women who could express themselves freely through clothing without drowning out their personalities. I just didn't believe I could be one of them."

Having her colors done brought her back to herself. It was a beginning. And her journey didn't stop there.

After they lost a baby, her husband sent her back for a style session — an act of love she still speaks about with gratitude. He knew she needed to feel supported in her body during that soul-wrenching season.

Sitting together during what was one of the lowest points in her life, Oriana and I talked, working through what she wanted to express about herself. I learned that growing up, she had been a tomboy — running with the neighbor boys, playing street ball in long shorts and oversized tees. She had tried trends and fads over the years, but none of them ever felt like her. When motherhood arrived, survival mode took over. Leggings, sports tees, messy bun.

"I called it good," she said. "But... I've always desired to be feminine. Being almost six feet tall and a twig, I've never known how to get there."

I eyed her with a mischievous smile. "When I look at you, I see a witch running through the forest with a billowing gown behind you." She still laughs about that.

Still, with those words, something in her clicked.

She suddenly understood her body wasn't the issue. Instead, she needed to change something in her mind — her mental permission to be who she really was. That began the next phase of her journey back to herself. Her transformation stunned even me, and I have seen many transformations over the years.

Years later, Oriana's sparkle is unmistakable. She dresses in honoring colors and styles that feel like her every day. She no longer cares about fads or other people's opinions. And while she might still have that tomboy streak, it's no longer in charge of what she wears. She's most often found in skirts, off-the-shoulder sweaters, and rust lipstick. Her husband now lovingly calls her his Forest Fairy. She is even publishing her first fantasy novel — a world that, fittingly, mirrors the same essence she uncovered through our work.

However, what matters most to Oriana isn't how she looks; it's what she passes on. I think of her as an example of brilliance because she's comfortable with herself in all the Facets, just as she is. She's not just self-empowered; she's a leader in her own way, who wants to empower others too.

"I love that I'm learning these things now," she said. "I can pass them down to my girls, so they don't hide their natural sparkle to please others."

This is brilliance: Not perfection or fearlessness, but self-knowledge that turns outward. Whether she's writing a book that could someday reach millions or raising her daughters to think for themselves, she's changing the world, one large or small step at a time.

If you've seen pieces of yourself in these stories — the doubt, the grief, the over-giving, the quiet longing — know this: You're on the right path. You're becoming. This book won't solve everything for you, but it will give you language, awareness, and questions you didn't know how to ask before. Sometimes, just these small-seeming elements can shift something inside you in a major way.

And this is why the work of the seven Facets matters. Your end reason is here, in this last section, when everything comes together. This is about the whole diamond, whose Facets each multiply the light from the others in a dazzling display.

FINDING YOUR UNIQUE BRILLIANCE

Everything you've read (or will read, if you're reading in your own sequence) in this book leads up to this point. And the first step is to remember what each Facet teaches: This isn't just about you. The world needs your unapologetic, authentic brilliance.

When you know who you are, you can change more than your own life. You can use that understanding to live more freely, love more honestly, and help others feel safe to do the same. You become a mirror — a guide — a light. Your own sparks can catch fire in others too. Who knows what amazing things can happen then?

It's time to find out.

What Dimmed Brilliance Looks Like

Brilliance is dimmed when any or all of your Facets remain rough and unpolished — or not polished enough. And once polished, if you're not regularly maintaining your diamond, it can lose luster too.

We've already gone through what this looks like, but let's tie it all together:

- **Identity Confusion** — You've lost sight of who you are beneath your roles and are shaping yourself around others' expectations.
- **Purpose Uncertainty** — You feel busy but not deeply fulfilled, unsure if your energy is moving in the right direction.
- **Low Self-Worth** — One critical voice outweighs a dozen affirmations and quietly shrinks your confidence.
- **Authenticity Struggles** — You adjust your personality to match the room instead of showing up consistently as yourself.
- **Indecisiveness** — You second-guess your instincts and delay movement while waiting for perfect clarity.
- **Scattered Focus** — You overcommit, overextend, and scatter your energy trying to hold everything together.
- **Unsupportive Relationships** — You stay in dynamics that drain you, or you silence yourself to preserve peace.

What an Integrated, Well-Polished Diamond Brings

Once you've attained this integrated mindset, you may notice:

- You recover from doubt faster than you used to.
- You recognize old patterns without being ruled by them.
- You're more aware of when you're shrinking and why.
- You still feel discomfort with attention, but you don't disappear inside it.
- You're learning to receive praise without deflecting it immediately.
- You feel more compassion for where you've been and greater steadiness where you are.

In this mindset, you'll be self-aware without self-judgment. Your confidence will spring from trust in yourself instead of from others' approval. You'll be present and potent in the moment and comfortable being seen even when it feels vulnerable, and you'll find you return quickly to peace after disruption.

How We'll Get There

The eight Sparks of Wisdom in this section will help you:

- Integrate everything you've learned into how you live, lead, and celebrate each transformation.
- Trust yourself to notice when you're slipping and gently redirect.
- Allow growth to feel imperfect, human, and ongoing.
- Let awareness replace shame when old fears resurface.
- Use your lived experience to support others with wisdom instead of over-giving.
- Recognize when old stories are resurfacing without letting them run the show.
- Shift your mindset faster using tools you now possess.
- Stay grounded in who you've become, not who you used to be.
- Share your brilliance in ways that feel aligned, generous, and sustainable.

You were never meant to polish one part of yourself while neglecting the others. You were designed to reflect light fully — not perfectly, but wholly. When your identity, purpose, voice, and relationships align, your brilliance stops feeling like effort and starts feeling like home.

Pressure, cut, and polish are just the beginning. Now it's time to let the diamond shine. Depending on where it's placed, it will reflect light differently. Yet no matter where it is, it always has light to share and multiply, making the world a brighter, more dazzling place.

LET YOUR BRILLIANCE GIVE OTHERS PERMISSION TO BE BRILLIANT TOO

In the other Facets, we talked about what it's like to light up in the spotlight compared to the urge to shrink the second it turns in your direction.

When you feel torn — wanting to shine but also terrified of being "too much" — it can be because you want to make sure no one else feels overshadowed. You dim your light so others stay comfortable.

You may tell yourself you're being kind, and yet, what if you are actually robbing others of the courage to shine?

Think about it for a moment. Many of us learned early on to make ourselves small to protect other people's feelings. We brush off compliments, downplay our talent, minimize our achievements, and avoid attention, even when we've earned it. All to make sure others aren't uncomfortable.

We don't speak up when we receive the wrong meal at a restaurant or when a service we paid for wasn't delivered. We quietly endure the inconvenience. And if someone else dares to advocate for themselves, we might even feel the urge to apologize for them.

We just smooth out discomfort automatically — like that's our job. But should it be?

Unfortunately, as we've seen, that approach doesn't honor our authenticity. And it doesn't set an example for others to honor theirs.

If your own authenticity makes someone else uncomfortable, that's not your responsibility to fix, soften, or absorb. Their reaction isn't a reflection of you — it's a result of their own insecurity. And you aren't responsible for carrying that weight.

Your brilliance doesn't take from anyone else. It gives other women permission to rise. When you stand in your fullness without apologizing, you become evidence of what's possible. If their self-worth is threatened because they are comparing themselves to you, it just indicates they need to do some work on that Facet in themselves — and that has nothing to do with you.

And worse, while you're focused on dimming your own light to make them feel more comfortable, someone else is waiting to see a brilliant, bold woman so they can finally believe they're allowed to shine, too. Which belief do you want to encourage — the one where you protect others from their own insecurities at your expense, or the one where everyone is confident and doesn't need protection?

I pick the second one. I hope you will, too.

*Dimming your light doesn't protect anyone — it only
hides the gifts God gave you. You were never meant to shrink.
When you shine, you give others permission to rise too.*

Reflect: Where in your life do you find yourself stepping back, minimizing, or apologizing for your gifts — and who taught you to do that?

Polish: Choose one moment this week when you would normally shrink, and do the opposite. Accept a compliment, speak up, share your idea, or stand confidently in your truth. Practice shining without apology.

RISE TO THE CALLING

When God nudges you into visibility, it's rarely because you feel ready. It's because someone else needs what your experience has taught you.

There are moments when an opportunity arrives — to speak, to lead, to share — and the immediate reaction is, "Why me?" That familiar doubt creeps in: "Am I qualified enough? Knowledgeable enough? Worthy enough to lead this conversation?"

And yet, we don't always have to be experts to speak on a topic. Often, the very topics we're asked to speak on are the ones God is still refining within us.

Preparing, studying, and stepping into those spaces becomes a spiritual exchange — a moment when growth happens on both sides. The lesson you teach becomes the lesson you embody, and the discomfort becomes clarity.

The most powerful affirmation doesn't come from applause, but from the woman in the audience who shares, "That was exactly what I needed to hear." Your presentation may not have been perfect in knowledge or expertise, but your authenticity and passion sparked a true connection.

Visibility stops being intimidating when it becomes sacred — a place where God transforms insecurity into impact. Through sincere dialogue, we shape our own experience into encouragement for others to grow.

Every time you look beyond the self-doubt and say yes, you step more fully into the woman God envisioned from the beginning.

When God calls you into the spotlight, it's not to show off your strength or credentials; it's to reveal His through you. Every time you say yes, you become the messenger of a sacred truth someone else is waiting to hear.

 **Reflect:** Have you ever been given an opportunity that scared you because it stretched you out of your comfort zone? What if those invitations aren't accidents but divine nudges showing you where your gifts are meant to shine?

 **Polish:** The next time you're asked to lead, speak, or share, resist the urge to shrink. Prepare your heart, say yes, and trust that God has already equipped you for the moment. Your willingness to step into the spotlight could be the answer to someone else's prayer.

RECEIVE COMPLIMENTS WITH GRACE

This one may seem small, but it is vital for mastering brilliance.

How many times has a compliment landed in your lap, only for you to swat it away like a fly?

"Oh, this old thing. I just threw it on."

"I was in the right place at the right time."

"It was a team effort."

"It's really not that big of a deal."

People-pleasers dismiss compliments to keep others from feeling uncomfortable. They downplay, deflect, and minimize because they see acknowledging compliments as braggy, full of themselves, or "too much." They feel safer shrinking than risking someone believing they think too highly of themselves.

I know there's a balance between humility and confidence, and it is sometimes better to err on the side of humility. And yet, when we're undermining ourselves, it's a different situation.

When you minimize yourself, you unintentionally teach others to treat your accomplishments, beauty, or effort as small. And after they obediently stop noticing what you do and take it for granted, you can feel unnoticed, unappreciated, and resentful.

It's time to break that cycle.

If you're not sure when you're undermining yourself versus being overly proud, I know it's the "safe" choice to just keep erring on the side of not making waves, but that won't change anything.

Instead, why not ask for help?

Find a trusted friend and assign her the task of calling you out when you do this — to lovingly remind you of things like, "It's okay to just say thank you." From the outside, she will have clear judgment. A coach can also guide you with this.

In fact, you may already be blessed to have someone like this in your life — if so, be grateful for that person, and listen to her! She is trying to help you.

When you receive a compliment, sometimes "thank you" is the bravest response you can give. Let others celebrate you and share in the joy of your achievements. It might just give them permission to celebrate themselves too.

Receiving a compliment with grace is not arrogance —
it is a refusal to disappear in order to keep others comfortable.

Reflect: When someone compliments you, what instinctive reaction rises first — acceptance, dismissal, or discomfort? Why do you think that is?

Polish: Today, choose to respond to every compliment with just two words: "Thank you." Pause. Smile. Let it land without explanation or deflection.

STEP BOLDLY INTO THE ROOM

True confidence begins when you stop waiting for acceptance and start owning the space God already placed you in. How do you achieve this? Like everyone else does — you just *do* it.

This might shock you, but even high-achieving leaders who feel confident on stage or in their work can feel terrified when walking into a room full of acquaintances. So, if you feel this way, you're in good company.

When you get invited into rooms with leaders you admire, instead of feeling honored, you may feel inadequate. You worry about saying the wrong thing, sounding unqualified, or taking up space you don't feel you've earned. You wear a name tag that reflects the role you currently hold, yet others are already treating you like the new woman you're becoming — and the disconnect can feel intimidating. Is what they see in you real?

To cope, you might scan the room, smile politely, find a corner to observe from, and wait for the right moment to belong. Once you're comfortable, you can talk for hours — but the initial step into visibility can make your heart race.

To counter this, remember why you're there.

The invitation is evidence of your worth, not an accident. When you show up — even if your voice is shaking or your heart is pounding — your courage brings you closer to the woman God designed you to be. When you hide in the corner, you miss the connection that could change your subconscious thoughts about yourself. When you stay silent, you forfeit the insight only you carry. When you assume you're the least qualified person in the room, you deny the growth that comes from stretching into it.

I've walked into rooms where others' perceptions of me felt bigger than my confidence. I've smiled, nodded, and wondered if someone would eventually realize I didn't belong. And yet, every time I chose to stay instead of retreating — every time I introduced myself first, asked a question, or contributed my thoughts — I gained confidence. Eventually, I realized I really did belong, and they really wanted me there.

The title on your name tag doesn't define you —
it's simply a placeholder for who you're becoming.
Every time you choose to show up,
you expand into the role you were meant to fill.

Reflect: Where in your life do you find yourself shrinking, even though others clearly see your light? What would happen if, just for today, you chose to believe their version of you — the one that's already worthy, capable, and called?

Polish: At your next event or gathering, set a small "visibility goal." Introduce yourself to one new person, share one idea, or take that group photo you'd normally avoid. You don't have to feel fearless to be visible — you just have to show up.

BE SEEN *AND* HEARD

In familiar spaces, you, like most women, are probably comfortable speaking freely. However, things change in a room with people you admire — or worse, with people who make you feel small. Suddenly, your voice feels shaky. You overthink every word, worry about asking a "stupid" question, or fear revealing that you don't know as much as you should.

And when the room is dominated by men, an old belief can still linger in the background — the subtle, unspoken message that women should be seen, not heard. Many leadership circles still carry this energy, even when the people are kind, capable, and well-intentioned.

These environments can make you hesitate or spend more time apologizing than contributing. And yet, the world is changing. Women are rising — leading, deciding, and building. We are shaping communities, businesses, families, and futures in ways we were not invited to generations ago.

You belong at every table where decisions are being made, and God did not gift you with intuition, insight, and leadership so you could stay silent.

In these stressful situations, your nervous system may naturally default to behaviors such as nurturing, smoothing, or avoiding conflict. You may seek harmony more than recognition. You may worry that speaking up will be misunderstood or judged.

And yet, your purpose requires you to speak up. The situation requires your contribution.

When you stay silent, something is lost. The question that could have shifted the conversation never gets asked. The perspective shaped by your experience never enters the room. Decisions move forward, missing your empathy, discernment, and long-term wisdom. Your voice isn't an optional accessory to the conversation. It forms part of the discussion's very architecture.

When you speak your mind in the rooms that once intimidated you, you don't just grow — you make space for every woman who comes after you to grow too. The world needs more women who speak with conviction, not apology.

Your voice deserves to be heard wherever
you can contribute something valuable.
Speaking up isn't disrespectful — it's evidence that
God placed wisdom within you that deserves to be heard.

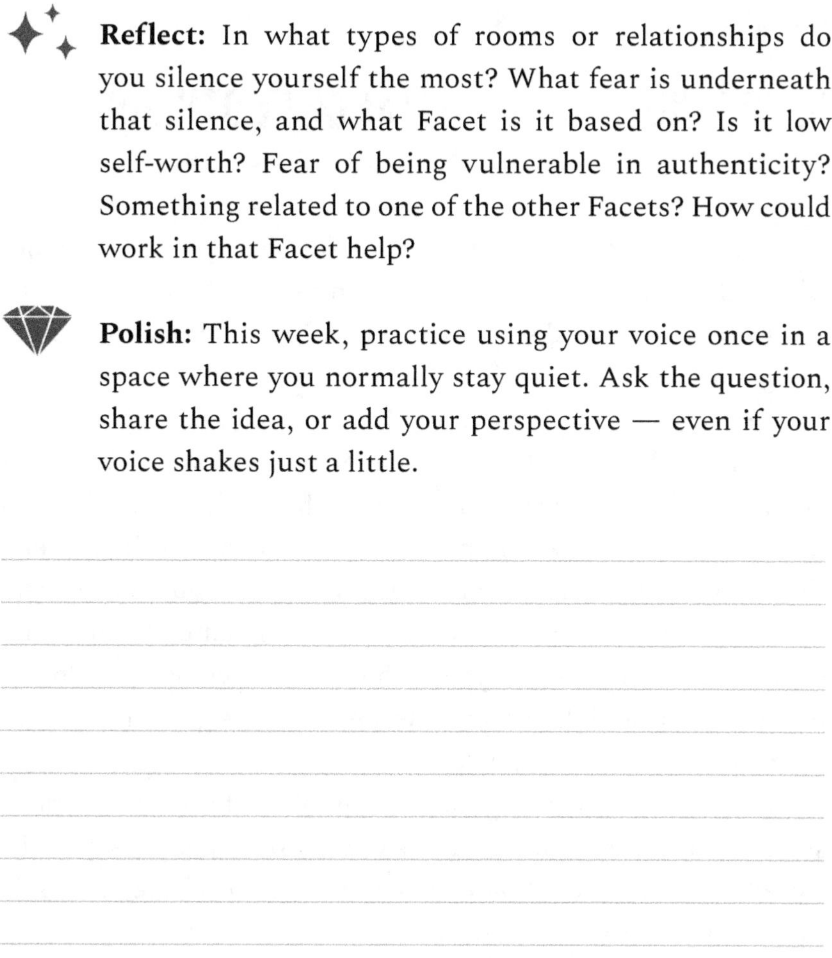

Reflect: In what types of rooms or relationships do you silence yourself the most? What fear is underneath that silence, and what Facet is it based on? Is it low self-worth? Fear of being vulnerable in authenticity? Something related to one of the other Facets? How could work in that Facet help?

Polish: This week, practice using your voice once in a space where you normally stay quiet. Ask the question, share the idea, or add your perspective — even if your voice shakes just a little.

HELP KINDLE THE BRILLIANCE IN OTHERS

Amanda, like me, had built a successful boutique — but somewhere along the way, it stopped feeling like hers. Her marriage was unraveling, and deep down, she felt the quiet pull for something *more*.

Beneath her confident smile lived an old memory and fear — one born the day of her high school graduation, when a terrible car accident nearly took her life and her ability to walk. Even though the odds worked in her favor and she had a full recovery, the mental damage from thinking about what could have been, as well as the pain during recovery and the adjustment of her altered self-image, all stayed in her subconscious. It followed her into adulthood like a shadow, creating the questions, *"Am I good enough? Can I handle this?"*

When an opportunity came to join her family's business, she hesitated. Change felt risky. What would people say if she closed her boutique? Would they see her as a failure, or would they see the faith & strength it took to walk away?

We prayed together through those questions, asking God for clarity and courage. I reminded her that obedience sometimes looks like letting go of what once worked to make room for what's next. Through every tear, every conversation about divorce, and every fear of change and starting over, we carried each other.

Looking back, I realized that the honor of being part of her support system was also training me for my next chapter. God was preparing both of us, refining our faith and resilience through each other's stories. Sometimes, the people we help heal become the mirrors that show us how far we've come.

*Walking alongside someone else's journey can reveal
the strength and faith you didn't know you had.*

Reflect: Who has God placed in your life that might be part of *your* preparation? Is there someone you're helping through a difficult season or someone who's unknowingly shaping your growth?

Polish: Reach out to that person today. Send a message, pray for them, or simply thank them for walking with you. Relationships built on faith and honesty are sacred gifts, and every one of them carries purpose.

SHARE WITHOUT SHRINKING

We've all had this moment. We're in a team discussion at work, with family around the dinner table, or with a group of friends or others, and a conversation topic surfaces — schedules, expectations, parenting styles, money, politics, or something else. Suddenly, the air shifts.

Smiles tense. Faces become guarded. Voices get louder or tighter. If everyone's tired or hungry, tempers are already fragile, threatening to explode.

You feel the moment in your body before your mind catches up. *Do I say what I really think, or smooth it over to keep the peace?*

For years, my instinct was to soften. To explain myself before anyone asked. To apologize in advance so no one felt uncomfortable.

I told myself I was being kind. But inside, something always tightened.

What I finally noticed was that silence didn't bring peace. It created distance — from myself. I saw this most clearly around the dinner table with family. That was when something clicked.

Not every difference of opinion requires defense. Not every uncomfortable moment means you're doing something wrong. And not every conversation is meant to end in agreement.

Learning to stay connected without self-betrayal changed everything. Now, when the conversation grows tense, I pause. I breathe. And I speak — calmly, honestly, without a disclaimer. Sometimes we find agreement, and that's great. And sometimes, we still disagree, and the conversation moves on unresolved. And that's okay too. Agreement or winning isn't the goal. Integrity is far more important.

You can listen without abandoning your perspective. You can disagree without attacking. You can speak clearly without over-explaining. You can respect another view without surrendering your own.

This is what it looks like when all the Facets work together.

Real conversation requires courage and kindness. If you're worried about creating more conflict than is necessary, you can pray before you speak, trusting God to guide your words, soften your tone, and prepare both hearts.

In brilliance, you come to acknowledge a truth: Self-abandonment, not disagreement, is what creates disconnection. You don't need to convince, win, or shrink. You merely need to stay grounded, honest, and open, allowing the relationship to either meet you there or reveal its limits. And either outcome is perfectly fine.

God can guide your words,
but you must be willing to speak them.

Reflect: Where do you most often soften, explain, or stay quiet to avoid tension — and what does it cost you internally when you do? When disagreement arises, are you protecting the authentic relationship, even if it's uncomfortable, or are you abandoning yourself to keep it comfortable?

Polish: This week, practice sharing one thought or opinion *without* a disclaimer. No "I'm sorry"; no "I'm sure this is stupid, but..."; and no "You'll probably disagree, but...." Just your voice, spoken with clarity and grace.

GOD IS YOUR BIGGEST FAN

There are places where your purpose comes alive — where your gifts flow, your voice is steady, your confidence strong. You step into a room full of strangers and feel strangely free. No expectations. No history. No old versions of you being projected onto who you are becoming. In those rooms, you shine without hesitation. You speak, lead, encourage, and feel completely aligned with what God created you to do. You feel amazing.

And then you step out of the spotlight and into your everyday life, and the loneliness hits. Those people closest to you don't understand that version of you. You seek connection with peers, friends, and others, wanting them to "get it," to understand... but they don't.

When that happens, the fire fueling you feels smaller. The pressure feels heavier. You suddenly become aware that others — even those you care deeply about — might be judging you, misunderstanding who you are, or quietly questioning why this work matters so deeply to you.

This is a difficult truth in leadership. Often, when you are standing in your highest calling, the people you love most simply aren't able to be there in the same way you are. It's not that they don't care. They just don't fully understand the version of you that is emerging.

Yet after the applause fades and the room empties, when you drive home with nothing but your thoughts, your purpose, and a hope that you made an impact, it may feel like you are alone, but you're not.

God is there. And He knows what others may not.

Your impact is real whether or not someone you love is sitting in the audience. Your purpose is valid even when others don't witness it firsthand. Your applause doesn't have to come from the crowd to be meaningful.

God doesn't just applaud your obedience.

He walks you to the stage, waits for you behind the curtain, and rides home with you in the silence.

Sometimes your greatest victories are witnessed by strangers,
not by the people you hoped would be there.
The lonely car rides home don't have to feel lonely.
Your calling is between you and God first.
He is with you — in every brilliant moment.

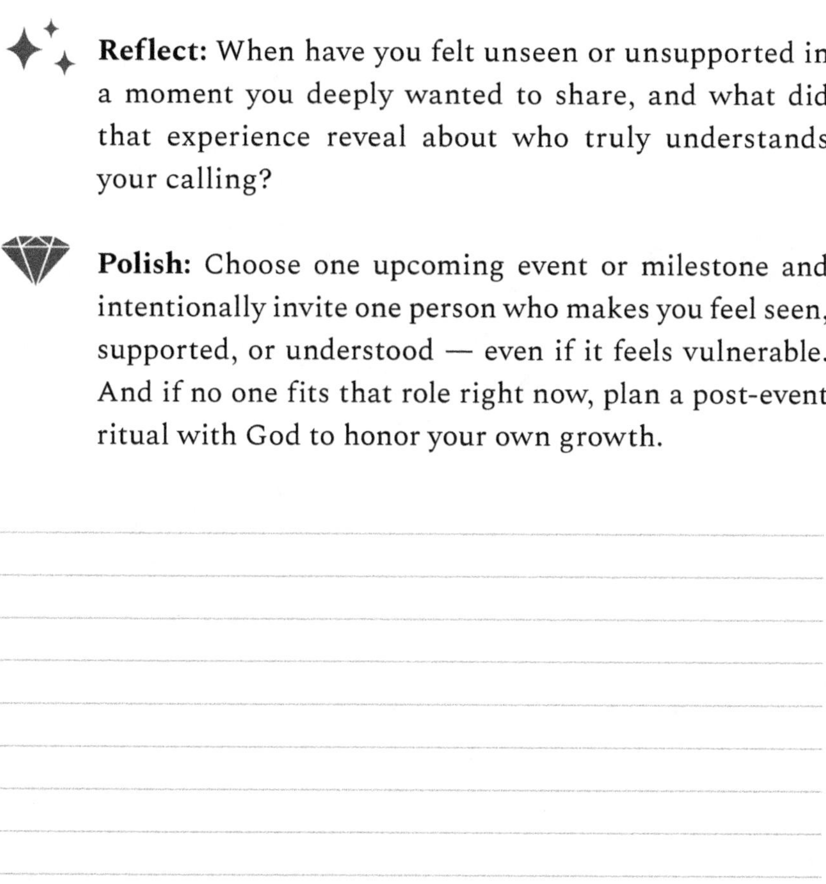

Reflect: When have you felt unseen or unsupported in a moment you deeply wanted to share, and what did that experience reveal about who truly understands your calling?

Polish: Choose one upcoming event or milestone and intentionally invite one person who makes you feel seen, supported, or understood — even if it feels vulnerable. And if no one fits that role right now, plan a post-event ritual with God to honor your own growth.

I WISH YOU THE DAZZLING FUTURE YOU DESERVE

As you reach the end of this book, my prayer is that you finally see the diamond you are becoming — the one God created with intention, brilliance, and purpose.

Just as a diamond is shaped one Facet at a time, so are you. You don't have to polish *everything* at once. You don't have to fix the whole story in a day. Together, we work gently and intentionally — one belief, one habit, one lie, one breakthrough at a time.

Life is constantly evolving. Our cells renew. Our circumstances shift. Our roles change. Seasons begin and end. And sometimes the very things that flip your world upside down become the moments that shape your greatest transformation. When you learn *how* to face those experiences with clarity, faith, and skill, you walk out stronger, steadier, and more ready for whatever God places in your path.

I know this journey can feel overwhelming at first. But as we walk through each Facet side by side, and as you revisit these Sparks and do the reflection and polishing actions/activities, you will start to feel more grounded, more equipped, and more confident as you step into every dream God whispers to your heart.

And if you ever struggle to find the right words to express what you're feeling — especially to the people you love — come back to this book as your starting point. These stories were written for you, but also for the women you will encourage, uplift, and empower along the way.

YOUR SMALL ACT OF THOUGHTFULNESS CAN KINDLE MORE SPARKS

Before you close this book, please take a moment to reflect:

- **Which Sparks tugged at your heart?**
- **Which Facets felt like they were written just for you?**
- **Who else came to mind as you read — someone who needs permission, hope, or a reminder that she is made for more?**

If this book blessed you, strengthened you, or awakened something inside of you, please take a moment to search for this book on Amazon and leave a review. Your words help other women find theirs.

Or go one step further — purchase a few copies, write a handwritten note inside, and gift them to your best friends, daughters, sisters, coworkers, or the woman God places on your heart. Because empowered women don't just rise... they lift others with them.

The greatest compliment you can ever give an author is to share her work. Thanks in advance for that gesture — from me and all the other women it will help empower.

And when you're ready to continue this journey beyond these pages, I'd love to invite you into my Diamond Coaching program.

This is where the real transformation begins — where we turn these Sparks and more into lasting breakthroughs. Together, we will polish your clarity, strengthen your confidence, and help you walk boldly into the purpose God designed you for.

You are not meant to do this alone. You don't have to guess your way forward. And you most definitely do not have to keep dimming your brilliance.

Let's walk this next chapter together.

Empowered women empower women. And you, my friend, are becoming a diamond.

XOXO,
Nicole

WITH GRATITUDE

First and always, I thank God. For the vision before the words. For the life experiences that shaped me. For His steady presence, guidance, and patience as this book unfolded exactly as it was meant to.

I am deeply grateful to Niche Press and Publisher Nicole Gebhardt, who could see my vision before I had language for it. She understood the heart and depth of the work I longed to do in the world and helped give my brand form with clarity and care. To her and her incredible team, especially my editor, Melanie — thank you for believing so fully in what was still becoming.

To my family, thank you for being my grounding and my *why*. And especially to my mom, who has been woven into so many chapters of my life. Thank you for your love, your strength, and the ways you shaped the woman I am today. I see you, I appreciate you, and I carry your love with me always.

And to Mark, Emma, Owen, and Brody, thank you for making me a wife and a mother, for stretching my heart, and for shaping me into the woman who could write these pages.

With love and gratitude,
Nicole 💎

ABOUT NICOLE

Nicole Lindhorst is a wife of more than twenty years to Mark, a proud mom of three — Emma, Owen, and Brody — and a life-long entrepreneur who has built multiple successful businesses with equal parts grit, grace, and faith.

Growing up in a divorced home taught Nicole the power of perseverance early on. She learned that hard work and heart — not circumstance — determine your direction.

Rooted in small-town values and driven by big dreams, Nicole has made it her mission to inspire others to rise above limitations and rediscover the brilliance within. Through her coaching, retreats, and her book *Becoming a Diamond*, she helps women navigate life transitions with confidence, purpose, and joy.

When she's not speaking, mentoring, or volunteering in her community, you'll find her traveling, sharing laughter with friends, reading a good book, or binge-watching Netflix with a cozy blanket, her mini schnauzer Baylee and a glass of wine. An outspoken believer in God, Nicole says her greatest passion is to remind others that faith is the foundation of every transformation and that we shine most brightly when we trust the One who created us to sparkle.

Nicole's message is simple but powerful: *You were never meant to shrink to fit in; you were created to shine.*

Contact

Website: NicoleLindhorst.com
Email: Nicole@NicoleLindhorst.com
LinkedIn: LinkedIn.com/in/Nicole-Lindhorst-23214b304
Instagram: @NicoleLindhorst3

Breakthrough Starts
WITH CLARITY

I see you. Your hard work has brought you to a level of achievement you're quietly proud of ... and a level of responsibility you feel barely able to juggle. Still, you keep doing all the things, never mentioning how alone, overwhelmed, and stuck you feel.

I want you to know **you're not alone**. And here's something that took me years to understand: **Transformation begins with knowing what's holding you back.** Knowing that, the next steps are simpler.

If this book has brought you some clarity, you're off to a good start. However, sometimes you need another person to help — someone who can see what you can't, who can reach through the blank (or muddy/cloudy) wall and pull you through to find out what's on the other side.

Using the Diamond Framework, **my 14-day Brilliant Start program will show you exactly what's holding you back so you can start moving forward — fast.** Even better: **As a reader, you'll receive a discount.**

Want to know more?

Start with my Diamond Assessment quiz, available at **NicoleLindhorst.com/Toolkit**, by scanning this QR code.